FORGIVENESS

CASCADE COMPANIONS

The Christian theological tradition provides an embarrassment of riches: from scripture to modern scholarship, we are blessed with a vast and complex theological inheritance. And yet this feast of traditional riches is too frequently inaccessible to the general reader.

The Cascade Companions series addresses the challenge by publishing books that combine academic rigor with broad appeal and readability. They aim to introduce nonspecialist readers to that vital storehouse of authors, documents, themes, histories, arguments, and movements that comprise this heritage with brief yet compelling volumes.

TITLES IN THIS SERIES:

FORGIVENESS

A Theology

ANTHONY BASH

 CASCADE *Books* • Eugene, Oregon

FORGIVENESS
A Theology

Cascade Books
An Imprint of Wipf and Stock Publishers
199 W. 8th Ave., Suite 3
Eugene, OR 97401

www.wipfandstock.com

ISBN 13: 978-1-4982-0148-3

Cataloguing-in-Publication Data

Bash, Anthony

    Forgiveness: a theology

    Cascade Companions 19

    xiv + 154 p. ; 23 cm. Includes bibliographical references and index.

    ISBN 13: 978-1-4982-0148-3

    1. Forgiveness 2. Title 3. Series

BT790.B08 2015

Manufactured in the U.S.A.   05/08/2015

Grateful thanks are given to Dr Imad N. Karam, Head of International Relations for *Initiatives of Change-UK* for permission to quote from the movie,
Beyond Forgiving, © 2013, of which he is Producer and Director.

Cover Art by Jim Linwood [CC BY 2.0 (http://creativecommons.org/licens-
es/by/2.0)], via Wikimedia Commons.

To Melanie
My best friend and most loyal critic
In deep gratitude, and with thanks to God

CONTENTS

PART 3   FURTHER QUESTIONS

ACKNOWLEDGMENTS

I AM, AS ALWAYS, grateful to friends and to conversation partners. To Geoffrey Scarre, in the Department of Philosophy at Durham University, I owe a continuing debt of gratitude. I also thank John Barclay in the Department of Theology and Religion at Durham University, for reading an earlier version of chapter 14. Hugh Firth has carefully read the book in draft twice, and given me incisive advice. The book is now much better for his critique. Ed Blancke has also read a draft of the book and made helpful suggestions. Above all, I thank Melanie, and our children, Hannah, Simeon, and Matthias, who have put up with me writing another book. They have used of me the computer term "buffering." By this, they mean that when I have been thinking about this book (as I often have been, even when I should have been fully engaged in family matters), it has sometimes taken me a long time to respond quickly or coherently even to ordinary and everyday matters. Their loyalty, love, support, and patience are more than anyone could ask for, and more than I deserve.

INTRODUCTION

IT IS STRANGE THAT interpersonal forgiveness, which is so widely regarded as fundamental to Christian identity and discipleship, is relatively neglected in academic theological literature. I cannot find modern books that offer a detailed theology of forgiveness set in a biblical context. Of course, there are popular books on forgiveness; some are better than others, and some, I think, are more pious than useful. On the whole, interpersonal forgiveness is remarkably under-researched. It is the Cinderella of theology. Though I am no Prince Charming, I hope this book will have a part in rescuing the theology of forgiveness from the obscurity of footnotes and of brief sections in books about related topics.

In contrast to the neglect of interpersonal forgiveness in modern theological writing, philosophers and psychologists are taking forward innovative work on forgiveness. To some extent and sometimes with different language, so also are lawyers and political scientists. Forgiveness is *exciting* if you are working in those fields. A lot of material is being published, and important new work is being undertaken.

Why is interpersonal forgiveness relatively understated among theologians?

I think one reason is because interpersonal forgiveness appears to be straightforward. However, it is in fact far from straightforward, both intellectually and practically. We have grown so familiar with the idea of interpersonal forgiveness that we pay lip service to it, without engaging with the fact that interpersonal forgiveness is hard to understand in its biblical setting. It is also the subject of considerable debate within the Christian Scriptures. Perhaps if I had not started to think about interpersonal forgiveness through an invitation to write about it in 2003, I would not now give so much time and thought to it.

Another reason why forgiveness is relatively understated among theologians is because interpersonal forgiveness tends to be overshadowed by books about related, and apparently weightier, matters, such as the atonement, divine justice, and divine forgiveness. These matters are not, I think, always necessarily weightier, although I agree they can sometimes be more complicated and more difficult to write about.

In addition, questions to do with the atonement, divine justice, and divine forgiveness have been at the center of theological debates and divisions for hundreds of years. They remain important topics of theological study for two reasons. First, because they have a critical place in the Christian understanding of salvation. Second, because they have sometimes had a divisive place in the history of the church and Christian thought. In contrast, people think interpersonal forgiveness is of peripheral concern, because it is apparently not one of the "great doctrines" of the Christian faith.

Perhaps people are right about the place of interpersonal forgiveness in terms of the narrative of Christian history, thought, and practice. What they may fail to take into account, however, is that the Synoptic Gospels (the Gospels of Matthew, Mark, and Luke) suggest that God does not forgive those who do not forgive others. Whether people recognize it or not, the Christian Scriptures regard the practice of interpersonal forgiveness as a prerequisite of salvation, and as evidence of salvation. To put it more boldly, this book explores how and when people loose themselves from God, from God's forgiveness, and from salvation if they do not forgive those who have wronged them. It also explores how interpersonal forgiveness *is* embedded in the "great doctrines" of the Christian faith, and how we can reaffirm its rightful place there.

We can perhaps go further. There is an unwritten and largely unrecognized narrative about un-forgiveness among individuals and communities that when properly told will, I suspect, point to perhaps more damage and division than have been caused by debates about the atonement and salvation. When I was a parish minister I never met a dying parishioner who regretted not spending more time at the office. I also did not meet any who took to their graves heartbreak about academic debates to do with the atonement. Sadly, however, all too many went to their graves grieving for friends and family from whom they were estranged through un-forgiveness.

I referred earlier to interpersonal forgiveness as the Cinderella of theology. I hope this book will help its readers see that it is in fact a Sleeping Beauty, ready to be woken by the kiss of a handsome prince. This Sleeping Beauty is intellectually fascinating, pastorally significant, and a Christian virtue. It is time for interpersonal forgiveness to be woken from the sleep in which it has been neglectfully left, and to take its rightful place in theology and practice. I hope this book will contribute to that task.

PART 1

CONCEPTUAL QUESTIONS

Chapter 1

FORGIVENESS AND HERMENEUTICS

HERMENEUTICS, MEANINGS, AND FORGIVENESS

ON MY FIRST DATE with Melanie (to whom I am now married), as we began our meal together, I said to her, "I have just written a paper on hermeneutics. May I discuss it with you?"

You may find this an unlikely question on a first date. Melanie certainly did. Nevertheless, the question, and the range of answers to the question, are worth talking about, even (or perhaps, especially!) on a date.

When I put the question to Melanie, she said, "What's 'hermeneutics'?" It is not surprising that she should have asked the question, as issues to do with hermeneutics are outside her own academic discipline and field of research.

In answer to Melanie, I said that hermeneutics are the range of ways and assumptions we might use to interpret texts, especially biblical texts. What I meant is that hermeneutics alert us to the fact that we make suppositions in order to interpret a text. One needs a "hermeneutic," that is, a framework of interpretive presuppositions, to understand any written text. I also said that hermeneutics are important because they give texts meaning; without hermeneutics, texts are no more than symbols in ink on a page.

The conversation about hermeneutics lasted the whole meal; "the rest," as is popularly said, "is now history."

In this book on forgiveness, I start with hermeneutics because the interpretive presuppositions we bring to writings about forgiveness in the New Testament, which from now on I refer to as "the Christian Scriptures," will shape the outcome of our reading. Some of the hermeneutics I will bring to our reading I have deliberately chosen; others I have deliberately excluded because I think they are mistaken or irrelevant. Unfortunately, I will be unaware of some of the hermeneutics I adopt, and in years to come I may regret how excluding them has skewed the reading that I offer in this book. I want to be "up front," as best I can be, about some aspects of how and why I read the texts as I do; you, the reader, may agree or disagree. So I am highlighting what I regard as important for explaining why I am approaching the interpretation of the Christian Scriptures on forgiveness in the ways I do.

I will now set out seven of the hermeneutical presuppositions that underlie much of the discussion about forgiveness in this book.

Forgiveness Is a Social Construct

We cannot describe what we mean by "forgiveness" and "forgiving" by reference to an objective notion of forgiveness, because no such objective notion exists. Rather, to speak of "forgiveness" and "forgiving" is to deploy language about socially constructed concepts that can best be understood against the cultural setting in which the concepts are used. This means we need to be sensitive to the context of the language and literature we are looking at. It would therefore not be surprising if words about forgiveness have one set of meanings in the Christian Scriptures, and another (but, of course, related) set of meanings in a different collection of writings or in popular, modern speech.

Forgiving Behavior Is Evidenced in a Variety of Ways

Forgiving behavior comprises a variety of different responses, with some of the responses more or less richly textured as behavior that we think is forgiving.[1] To accept an apology that is offered with a gift of a bunch of flowers as an expression of contrition is probably to forgive; so also (just about) is for a mother to receive and accept a surly grunt (that sounds like the word "sorry") from a teenager who has been rude to her. In contrast, some patterns of behavior are related to what we understand to be forgiveness or forgiving behavior but they do not have enough of a "family resemblance"[2] to forgiveness and forgiving behavior for us properly to call them "forgiveness" or "forgiving behavior." So if we say, for example, that the "hard center" of forgiveness is not holding against another person the wrong that person has done to us, we might want to say that the effect of ignoring a wrong is akin to forgiveness but not truly forgiveness, notwithstanding that the outcome in both cases, pragmatically speaking, is often similar.

1. Bash, *Just Forgiveness*, 35–39.

2. The phrase is Wittgenstein's in *Investigations*, §67. The phrase refers to what is thought to be connected by one identifying, common feature but which is in fact connected by overlapping similarities, with no one similarity common to all examples.

The Christian Scriptures Are an Anthology

The Christian Scriptures are not one book but, as they stand today in most Christian traditions, an anthology of twenty-seven books, written by a variety of different authors. In different ways, the books are seeking to make sense of the "Christ-event" (that is, the significance of the life, death, and resurrection of Jesus Christ) for those to whom the individual books were written. It is also important to add that the anthology of books that now comprise the Christian Scriptures was written during the course of the first century CE, probably beginning about the midpoint of that century, and perhaps into the early part of the second century CE. This means that they may have been written over about a sixty-year period, with different authors and at different stages in the development of the early Christian church.

One implication of these straightforward statements is that what we read about forgiveness in the Christian Scriptures might not necessarily be self-consistent. In other words, there might be a variety of understandings as to what it means to forgive, because different authors may have different interpretations of and approaches to forgiveness. Certainly, we cannot assume that there is "one voice" on forgiveness in the Christian Scriptures. Additionally, the twenty-seven books may also point to a change, or development, of understanding about forgiveness in the period during which they were written. We cannot assume that, in the first century of the church, the notion of what it means to forgive, and why and when it is right to forgive, remained unchanged.

The Chronological Order of the Composition of the Christian Scriptures Influences How We Interpret Them

Many think that we should begin with the Gospels to identify the earliest Christian traditions about forgiveness.

However, the Gospels, as we now have them, contain material that is almost certainly the result of some years of development, editing, and reflection, and are based on traditions that were at first circulated orally. Of course, the Gospels may well contain elements of what Jesus said and taught about forgiveness, but we cannot be sure what precisely is "original" (the word scholars often use in this connection is "authentic") and what may be later developments.

We should note too that each of the Gospels is a work of theological reflection in its own right. It is a mistake to see any of the Gospel writers as no more than uncritical collectors of material that has been put into a book called a "gospel." When it comes to forgiveness, what each of the Gospel writers includes appears deliberately to have been chosen and even, to some extent, shaped to reflect that Gospel writer's own theological purpose. For example, Luke's theology of forgiveness is different from Matthew's, and Matthew's different from Mark's. Each Gospel can be read on its own as a discrete work of theology, and, as we shall see clearly later in this book, a careful comparison of one Gospel with another will reveal significant differences of emphasis, approach, and understanding when it comes to forgiveness.

Given that what we now have in the Gospels has very likely been developed from earlier oral and written sources, and then edited, is it possible to know accurately what Jesus said, and can we disentangle what Jesus said from later additions that are now part of the Gospels? Scholars have developed criteria for identifying what they believe can point us to what they call the "authentic sayings" of Jesus. I think it is fair to say that their efforts can now be regarded as a failure.[3] We therefore cannot be certain about what Jesus

3. Hooker, "Christology"; Barbour, "Tradition-History"; Hooker, "Wrong Tool"; Allison, "It Don't Come Easy."

did or did not say. We return shortly to whether this last point is significant.

Despite what is popularly assumed, the writings of Paul the Apostle are, almost certainly, the earliest of the writings in the Christian Scriptures. Disconcertingly, therefore, if we want to identify the earliest writings on forgiveness in the Christian Scriptures, we should look at Paul's letters and not the Gospels.

But which are Paul's letters? Of the thirteen letters attributed to Paul, only seven are regarded as almost certainly coming from him. The seven are Romans, Galatians, Philippians, 1 Corinthians, 2 Corinthians, 1 Thessalonians, and Philemon. Even of these, some may be compilations of what he wrote, put together by later editors, with the occasional passage doubted as to whether it is genuinely Pauline (e.g., 2 Cor 6:14–7:1). Varying degrees of doubt exist about the six "disputed" letters, though probably, the letters in the form that we now have them either are based on earlier, and now lost, genuine letters of Paul or are perhaps letters written by another writer seeking to follow, and develop, the theology of Paul. They address new situations and circumstances faced by Christian churches after the death of Paul. The six "disputed" letters are Ephesians, Colossians, 2 Thessalonians, 1 Timothy, 2 Timothy, and Titus.

The Cultural Context of the Christian Scriptures Influences How We Interpret Them

It is important to be alert to the cultural and social context in which the Christian Scriptures have come to us. Paul wrote as someone from within the Jewish tradition; he was a Hellenized Jew, which means that the way he lived his Jewish faith and practice was, to some extent, the result of more than three centuries of Jewish adaptation to the Hellenized culture of the Roman Empire. Paul's first language was Greek, not Hebrew, and, in his letters, he quotes from the Septuagint, the Greek translation of the Old Testament (which from now on I shall refer to as "the Hebrew Scriptures") that was in widespread use by Greek-speaking Jews. Of course, there were many gradations of Jewish adaptation to Greek culture throughout the Roman Empire. Perhaps it is best to say that in seeking to understand and interpret Paul's writings, we must remember two things: first, that Paul was both rooted in Judaism and rooted, in some measure, in Greek culture; second, that both Jewish culture and Greek culture shaped how and why he wrote what he did. It is therefore very likely that Paul knew, and would have been influenced by both Greek and Jewish patterns of thought about forgiveness. We might expect to see these patterns influence how he explores and interprets a Christian approach to forgiveness.

It is more complicated when it comes to the Gospels. Jesus is rooted in "Palestinian Judaism," Judaism that was more traditional than the Judaism of many parts of the Roman Empire outside Palestine. What Jesus said about forgiveness comes out of that Palestinian setting. However, the Gospels are probably addressed to and, importantly, made relevant for communities whose cultural and religious setting is different. In effect, the Gospels have been made relevant for people in a different situation from those to whom Jesus spoke, and address new questions that the early church, but not Jesus's former hearers, faced. Luke's Gospel is an obvious example: Luke was writing for a Greek reader, Theophilus. The Gospel seems to reflect the perspective and concerns of Gentile (non-Jewish) Christians, with Luke adapting for a different setting material about Jesus, what he said, and what he did, that formerly came out of a Jewish cultural context. Matthew's Gospel seems to be addressed to Jewish Christians whose relationship with Palestinian

Judaism was becoming increasingly detached; Matthew seems to have shaped his material to reflect that increasing detachment. These observations mean that, when it comes to forgiveness, it is difficult to identify with certainty what Jesus said and taught because, in the way the material now appears, it has been reshaped and reworked for a culturally and socially different audience.

This is probably less troubling than at first it seems. I suspect that the question whether we can know what Jesus said about forgiveness is inseparable from the question the Gospel writers were asking, namely, what is the significance of what Jesus said about forgiveness. The former question is relatively uninteresting and one-dimensional; the latter sets Jesus's teaching in an interpretive framework that is cultural, contextual, and theological. To put it simply: what someone may have said is of little "cash value" unless set within an interpretive frame. So long as the Gospel writers were no more than interpreting and applying what Jesus had said to their own situations (rather than writing, in effect, fiction) they were doing what many preachers and teachers do today: they were making the Jesus traditions relevant and applicable to their audiences.

The Christian Scriptures Are Not Exhaustive

The Christian Scriptures disclose many debates, sometimes conducted in a bad-tempered and combative way, as the writers tried to make sense of the Christ-event. There are often disagreements; there are even rows and schisms. If one reads the Christian Scriptures carefully, there is no sense that the last word has been said on the subject matter of the debates, or even that unanimity had been reached. Moreover, I do not think that theological reflection and development stop with the completion of the written, Christian Scriptures. So, when it comes to forgiveness in the twenty-first century, for example, there is therefore no reason why we should not continue to reflect on the meaning of the Christ-event. We may perhaps thereby develop some new insights into what it means to forgive.

All Sources of Learning May Inform Christian Theology

Lastly, it seems to me self-evident that God gives wisdom and insight to all people, whether they are from a faith tradition or not, and, if they are from a faith tradition, whether they are from the Christian faith tradition or not. There is no reason why the wisdom and insight of all people should not enrich a theological reading of the Christian Scriptures. The wisdom and insight may be important for addressing new questions about forgiveness, or suggesting new approaches. They may also enhance and enrich the approaches to forgiveness we find in the Christian Scriptures, rather than be in conflict with them. In other words, modern wisdom and insight may enlarge the approach to forgiveness we find in the Christian Scriptures, and contribute to a better understanding of why, and how, and when people may forgive. Obviously we will also need to discern to what extent contemporary insights cohere with and even enrich the insights of the Christian Scriptures on forgiveness.

As you will see as you read this book, I have benefited much from the insights of philosophers, political scientists, psychologists, and lawyers when it comes to forgiveness. Where I can, I have sought to integrate those views into a theology of forgiveness. What I will suggest about forgiveness in this book addresses twenty-first-century questions and discussion about forgiveness. It also addresses how forgiveness was explored and formulated in the Christian Scriptures in the early years of Christianity. What I am also seeking to do is to formulate a theology of forgiveness through mutual dialogue and engagement with both modern and ancient material.

QUESTIONS

1. What are hermeneutics and why are they important?
2. Which hermeneutical presuppositions are adopted in this book? Which others could have been included?

Chapter 2

THE DISCOVERY OF FORGIVENESS

JESUS AND FORGIVENESS

HANNAH ARENDT WROTE THAT Jesus is the "discoverer" of forgiveness.[1] Arendt based this observation on her understanding of the Jewish traditions about forgiveness in the Hebrew Scriptures. She apparently thought that the Hebrew Scriptures referred only to God's forgiveness, and that in the Hebrew Scriptures there is next to nothing about interpersonal forgiveness. It is Jesus, she says, who introduced the idea of interpersonal forgiveness into theological and ethical thought.

In my view, Arendt is mistaken that Jesus is the "discoverer" of forgiveness. As we shall see, before the time of Jesus and despite the lack of widely used and explicit language in ancient cultures to describe interpersonal forgiveness, forgiving behavior was widespread, and probably universally practiced.

1. Arendt, *Human Condition*, 238.

Forgiveness in Ancient Jewish Traditions

In the Hebrew Scriptures, the focus is undoubtedly on divine forgiveness. Forgiveness was the gift of God to people who were members of the Jewish covenant community who kept the law.[2] God's forgiveness restored people to grace and to God.[3] Forgiveness was an act of God in respect of sins. Sacrificial offerings for wrongdoing were only for ritual or moral impurity through defilement or contagion,[4] and there were no offerings for sins deliberately and intentionally committed. There was also no "guarantee" that God would forgive repentant wrongdoers: forgiveness was a gift of grace, given if and when God wished.[5]

Several verbs are used for God's forgiveness and they all point to a gift that God alone gave to people. The Hebrew verb that is most close to what we mean today by "to forgive" is *salah*. There is no corresponding noun. Another verb, *rasah*, though strictly not meaning "to forgive," refers to God being pleased with or accepting something favorably. In Lev 26:41, 43, *rasah is* used of God being satisfied with amends that people make for the sins they have committed. Three other words point to divine forgiveness: *nasa'* (to lift or carry away), *hata'* (to expiate, cleanse, or free from sin), and *khipph̲er* (to appease, pacify, or atone).

Interpersonal forgiveness is scarcely ever explicitly referred to in the Hebrew Scriptures, so there is no pattern of language about interpersonal forgiveness to point to.[6] Even so, forgiving behavior (by which I mean actions, accompanied with remorse, apology, contrition, or sorrow,

2. Sakenfield, "Problem," 327–28.

3. Milgrom, *Leviticus 1–16*, 245.

4. See Lev 5:1–9, e.g.

5. E.g., Jonah 3:10 and, from the Christian Scriptures, Acts 8:22.

6. Johansson, "Who Can Forgive?," and Morgan, "Mercy."

which usually result in restored relationships) did take place. It is not right to suggest that Jewish people before the time of Jesus were unforgiving: of course men and women thought they could forgive one another, and they did. In Gen 50:15–21, for example, Joseph's brothers tried to ensure Joseph forgave them.

From the Hebrew Scriptures, we see that God forgave sins. Human beings, if they did forgive, did not forgive *sins*. What we now mean by "interpersonal forgiveness" is only rarely referred to as "forgiveness." I suspect the ancient Jews would have thought that it would have been impertinent, perhaps even blasphemous, to claim for human beings an action that was regarded as characteristic of God's atoning mercy. This explains why Joseph apparently refused to forgive his brothers, saying in Gen 50:19, "Am I in the place of God?" It also helps explain why in Mark 2:7 the scribes objected that Jesus forgave a paralytic's sins: they thought Jesus to be a human being, and no more than a human being.

Interpersonal Forgiveness in Ancient Greek Traditions

Greek ethics did no`t recognize forgiving behavior as virtuous, or even recognize interpersonal forgiveness as a discrete category of behavior.[7] However, in pre-Christian Greek literature there is evidence that people forgave one another. One Greek set of words, based on the root *syngn-*, commonly expressed the idea of excuse, pardon, allowance, and forgiveness.[8] However, the ancient Greek idea of forgiveness is different from contemporary ideas of forgiveness, because forgiveness was then usually preceded, not by

---

7. Griswold, *Forgiveness*, 14, and Konstan, *Before Forgiveness*, 16.

8. Griswold, *Forgiveness*.

confession and apology, as is now generally the case in the Judeo-Christian tradition, but by "excuse or exculpation."[9]

Other Examples of Interpersonal Forgiveness

There are examples of forgiveness outside the Jewish and Greek traditions. For example, there is evidence of forgiveness and forbearance in ancient Chinese culture.[10] Written evidence for the Mahayana Buddhist idea of forgiveness developed around the time of the Christian Scriptures. It celebrates the virtue of equanimity, including forgiveness, which leads to spiritual freedom. There is even evidence that some higher primates engage in behavior that appears to provide a resolution of conflicts and to result in reconciliation.[11]

Implications

I think it is likely that interpersonal forgiveness has always been universally practiced in one form or another, and perhaps even has its roots in human evolutionary development. Nevertheless, we must not understate the achievement of the writers of the Christian Scriptures. For the Christian Scriptures offer the earliest recorded and the earliest sustained exploration and celebration of forgiving behavior as a discrete pattern of behavior; the Christian Scriptures are also the earliest sustained celebration of forgiving behavior as virtuous. To clarify: forgiving behavior has always been practiced; however, it had not previously been detached from related behaviors, given its own name and form, and celebrated as a virtue in quite the same way as it is in the Christian Scriptures.

9. Konstan, "Assuaging Rage," 17.
10. Harbsmeier, "Forgiveness and Forbearance."
11. De Waal, "Chimpanzee."

As we shall see, it seems very likely that it is Jesus who first extensively developed Jewish thinking about interpersonal forgiveness in this new way, accelerating a development that is in evidence in Judaism in the second and first centuries BCE.[12] In effect, he synthesized, labeled, and enhanced a pattern of behavior that is implicit in what it means to love one's neighbor, such as found in Lev 19:18 and Sir 28:2. Semantically speaking, as a result of what Jesus said, people became forgivers in a way and to an extent that was unparalleled before then.

Perhaps it is not surprising that this important adaptation of the way people thought about forgiveness took place from within the Jewish tradition. As I have said, in the Jewish tradition, forgiving was what God did in respect of the sins of people. It is not an enormous leap of imagination to say that human beings, who in the Hebrew Scriptures are said to be in the image of God, are to strive to live in a way that reflects God-likeness. For in the same way that the followers of Jesus are to "be perfect" because their "heavenly Father is perfect" (Matt 5:48), so they are to be forgivers, because their heavenly Father is forgiving.

Arendt is therefore mistaken to say that Jesus is the "discoverer" of forgiveness. Quite simply, he is not. However, what Jesus did was to highlight, explore, and celebrate forgiveness as a discrete expression of virtuous behavior in enhanced ways—ways the full extent of which are still being explored today.

---

12. See, e.g., Sir 28:1–5 (an early second-century BCE deuterocanonical text). The Jewish scribe ben Sira of Jerusalem wrote Sirach. Sirach is not part of the Hebrew Scriptures and exists now only in Greek translation as part of the Septuagint. On the connections between Sirach and Jesus's teaching on interpersonal forgiveness, see Chadwick, *The Church*, 28; Corley, *Sirach*, 79; Snaith, *Ecclesiasticus*, 139–40.

THE "DISCOVERY" OF FORGIVENESS AND THE JEWISH LAW

Jesus spoke and taught as a Jewish teacher of the Jewish law. He summarized the Jewish law as being to love God and to love one's neighbor.[13] This summary is the basis of Christian ethics in the Christian Scriptures.[14] Although Jesus does not explicitly say this, to forgive others is one of the ways to love one's neighbor.

The double emphasis—on love as the basis of ethics and on interpersonal forgiveness as an important expression of love—explains, I suggest, the differing prominence that love and interpersonal forgiveness are given in the Christian Scriptures. As we shall see, in the Gospel of Matthew and the Gospel of Luke, for example, Jesus refers frequently to forgiveness; in the Gospel of John and 1 John, the emphasis is on love. It is not that love and forgiveness are in conflict; they are different starting points for describing virtuous behavior, the former being a summary and the latter an example.

Jesus gives a different summary of the Jewish law in Matt 7:12 and Luke 6:31 (echoing Lev 19:18, 34). The summary is one of the expressions of what is generally known as "the Golden Rule," an apothegm (a pithy saying or maxim) that is independently found in many secular and religious ethical systems. The "Rule" is that people should not treat others in ways they would not want to be treated themselves (this reflects the approach of Lev 19:18); it is also that they should treat others as they would like others to treat them (expanding the implications of Lev 19:34). One implication

13. Matt 22:35–40, Mark 12:28–34, Deut 6:4–5, Lev 19:18.

14. When Paul refers to "the law of Christ" in Gal 6:2, he probably means "Jesus's summary of the Jewish law as being to love God and to love one's neighbor." See also Jas 1:25; 2:21.

of the Rule is that if people hope to be forgiven, they should forgive those who wrong them.

As we shall see, Jesus says that divine forgiveness and interpersonal forgiveness are co-dependent, and that those who are unforgiving toward others take themselves away from God's forgiveness. We might add that, just as judgment is without mercy toward those who show no mercy (Jas 2:13), so God's judgment is without forgiveness toward those who show no forgiveness to others. At this point, we can borrow Paul's words in Rom 11:22 to note the "kindness" and the "severity" of God: God is kind and forgiving toward those who forgive others, but God is severe toward those who do not forgive others—unavoidably so, because they have cut themselves off from God's forgiveness. They seal their own fate by their un-forgiveness.

Which reasons do the Christian Scriptures give to explain why unforgiving people cut themselves off from God's forgiveness? One reason, which I discuss in chapter 10, is that if victims are unforgiving toward those who wrong them, they will not also be in a frame of mind to seek or receive God's forgiveness. It is not that unforgiving people forfeit the grace of God's forgiveness that once was theirs: it is that by their own actions, and while they continue in un-forgiveness, they take themselves away from and out of the grace of God, and so are no longer able to receive it.

There is, however, another reason, which we can set within a Jewish context from the Hebrew Scriptures. Expressed simply, those who disobey the ethics of the covenant (such as to love their neighbors) put themselves, like "tax collectors and sinners," outside the grace of the covenant. Those who want to return, seek to return, and return in penitence are welcomed back, as was the Prodigal Son (Luke 15:11–32); however, if they remain unforgiving, they will neither seek nor want to return, because they are repudiating the basis on which they can return.

Jesus said he did not abolish the Jewish law, but left it in place and "fulfilled" it (Matt 5:17), that is, he fully brought out its purpose and intention with definitive interpretations. Thus, the ethics of Jesus are set in the context of the Jewish law, and are a development and reinterpretation of it. There is continuity between the ethics of the Hebrew Scriptures and the ethics of the Christian Scriptures, for their lineage is the same. We see again that Jesus is not the "discoverer" of interpersonal forgiveness; rather, he gave form to and (in the case of interpersonal forgiveness) particularized what is implicit in the Hebrew Scriptures.

DEFINITIONS OF FORGIVENESS

Arendt's suggestion that Jesus is the "discoverer" of forgiveness conceals another important, but doubtful, assumption about forgiveness. The assumption is that Jesus discovered something that can be easily identified and agreed upon. In other words, Arendt is assuming that forgiveness can be described and even defined in such a way that we can say with certainty both what forgiveness is and what forgiveness is not.

We may think that, on a day-to-day basis, we know what it means to forgive and that it would be easy to come up with a definition of forgiveness. However, a little thought, especially in the context of "real life" issues, may disclose that forgiveness is rather more subtle and more complex than perhaps we realize, and that to come up with a definition may be tantalizingly difficult. If you are in doubt about the fluidity of what we mean by forgiveness, consider, for example, the following three imaginary scenarios.

Scenario 1

Suppose I ask you to lunch. You are my best friend. You forget the invitation. I sit and eat lunch on my own, feeling sorry for myself. Should I forgive you? Some would say that to speak of "forgiveness" in such a scenario verges on "overkill," as what we are talking about is not wrongdoing on your part but rudeness, carelessness, and thoughtlessness. I might instead just shrug my shoulders, and choose to overlook your thoughtlessness, perhaps saying to myself, "She often forgets to look in her diary. I just have to get used to it."

Scenario 2

Imagine the same lunch invitation. You are absorbed in a difficult matter in the office; the problem you are dealing with is so interesting that you do not notice the time. An hour later you notice, and so you call to tell me a "white lie" to the effect that you have been "delayed at the office." It is true that you have been delayed, but you choose to omit to say that the delay is of your own making, due to forgetfulness. I later find out the truth, and I am hurt and angry. Should I forgive you?

There are several ways of approaching this question. If a lie has been told and if it is always morally wrong to lie, I might forgive you for lying to me. However, I might think that telling a "white lie" is not a moral wrong but a social convention for avoiding embarrassment. If so, some would say that the question of forgiveness is irrelevant, because we can forgive only moral wrongs. However, I might think that forgiveness is wide enough to include acts and omissions that are not moral wrongs: I could then choose to forgive the "white lie." Even then, I might decide not to bother even with thinking about forgiving you for the "white lie" on the basis of "proportionality," saying that forgiveness should be reserved for serious matters, and should not be offered if I am no more than irked by manipulation of truth for social convenience.

Scenario 3

Imagine the same lunch invitation again. I arrive a few minutes early, and as I sit waiting for you, I am mugged, and my wallet and cell phone stolen. Afterwards, I am badly affected by the robbery and suffer shock. I become agoraphobic and eventually cannot leave my house to go to work. I lose my job; in consequence, I cannot keep up the mortgage payments on my apartment. The mortgage company forecloses, and I have to move to social housing. A year later, the thief is traced by the police and sentenced to a year in prison. After sentencing, the thief shouts at the judge and says (in rather less refined language than what follows) that there is no reason why he should not have stolen what he wanted because the victim is rich and can easily buy replacements. I read about this outcry in the local press and decide, nevertheless, to forgive the thief, notwithstanding his lack of remorse, because I consider it to be my "Christian duty."

Some might applaud my action and say that it models true forgiveness, because it offers a new start to an undeserving wrongdoer. Others might insist that forgiveness can only truly be offered if first there are remorse and contrition, and perhaps even reparation. Otherwise, they might say, forgiveness becomes a rogues' charter that entitles wrongdoers to expect to be let off the consequences of what they have done; this kind of "forgiveness," they might add, also wrong-foots victims who, if they believe it is right to forgive the unrepentant, have to deny their sense of outrage about the wrongdoing to comply with a supposed duty to forgive the unrepentant.

THE PARAMETERS OF FORGIVENESS

I hope the examples above illustrate that the boundaries of forgiveness can be difficult to describe, and that it is not always obvious when one should or should not offer forgiveness. In short, forgiveness is not at all straightforward and, even when people are sure that they can or should offer forgiveness, forgiveness can be difficult to put into practice.

I do not think it is possible to come up with a definition of forgiveness, and I do not think the Christian Scriptures are unequivocal when it comes to forgiveness. Ludwig Wittgenstein says of definitions and the meaning of words that words do not have "sharp" boundaries; rather they have "blurred edges."[15] This can make formulating definitions of concepts next to impossible. To use Wittgenstein's terminology again, we can say of "forgiving" and "forgiveness" that they are "uncircumscribed," that is, without definitive boundaries.[16]

Not unexpectedly, therefore, no one seems to have managed to come up with a definition of forgiveness on which all people agree. Definitions of forgiveness seem to go one of two ways. Some are over-simplifications that fail to do justice to the complexity of a subject. Butler's definition of forgiveness as "forswearing resentment," the shortcomings of which we consider in detail in chapter 4, is an example of this sort of definition. Other definitions are convoluted and end up reading like statutory enactments, the sort of thing a lawyer might write: dry, lifeless, and

15. *Investigations*, §§76, 71.
16. Ibid., §65.

sometimes even baffling. The result in both cases is that no one is very much the wiser.

Instead of offering a definition of forgiveness in this book, I will identify, as best I can, the variegated parameters of forgiveness. At the least, a theology of forgiveness, even if it does not offer definitive answers about forgiveness, should be set out in a way to offer an appropriate intellectual and moral framework for reflecting theologically on forgiveness, and on its nature and limits. What I hope I will be able to do is to identify the "complicated network of similarities, overlapping and criss-crossing"[17] that is forgiveness in the Christian Scriptures, and see the network's relationship to forgiveness as it was understood in the first century CE and as it is now understood in the twenty-first century after two millennia of reflection.

QUESTIONS

1. In which senses is Jesus the "discoverer" of forgiveness?

2. Discuss this statement: "Jesus is not the 'discoverer' of interpersonal forgiveness; rather, he gave form to and (in the case of interpersonal forgiveness) particularized what is implicit in the Hebrew Scriptures."

3. Discuss the range of behaviors that may be forgiven. Explain why they may be forgiven.

4. Can we define forgiveness? Why or why not?

17. Ibid., §66.

Chapter 3

FORGIVENESS

LANGUAGE, MODELS, AND METAPHORS

LANGUAGE ABOUT FORGIVENESS

As LANGUAGE DEVELOPS, WE sometimes adapt existing words, and give them new meanings. Consider, for example, the words "gay" ("cheerful"; or "homosexual") or "spoiler" ("someone who spoils something"; or "the flap on an airplane to reduce the airplane's speed"; or "a candidate in an election who has no chance of winning but whose entry into the election is to thwart the chances of another candidate"; or "information about a plot that discloses a surprise").

Changes in language about forgiveness similarly took place in the first century CE in the Greek-speaking parts of the early Christian church. The two existing secular Greek words that included the idea of interpersonal forgiveness in their semantic range were *synginōskō* and a related noun *syngnōmē*. The early Christians chose not to express their new understanding of interpersonal forgiveness with these words because, I think, they wanted to avoid the risk of conflating the secular Greek and the Christian approaches to forgiveness. Instead, the early Christians adapted *aphiēmi* and *aphesis*, existing words for divine forgiveness from the Septuagint. They also adapted everyday, secular Greek words, which before then had not obviously meant forgiveness, to express what they wanted to say about the essence of Christian forgiveness.

Aphiēmi **and** Aphesis

Aphiēmi and *aphesis* commonly mean to let go, leave, allow, permit, and so on. In the Septuagint (and of course in the Christian Scriptures, too), these words are also used of God forgiving sins. Some writers of the Christian Scriptures use these words to describe the way individuals might forgive those who commit interpersonal wrongs. There was already precedent for this, as we have seen when we discussed Sir 28:2.

There are two ways victims can "let go." The most obvious way is for victims to let go of the personal consequences—psychological, emotional, legal, and so on—of having been wronged. Paul declined to do this, for example, after having been wrongfully beaten and imprisoned, and would only do so after he had received a public apology (Acts 16:35–40). The other way victims can let go is for victims, in some way, to "release" wrongdoers from the wrong. John 20:23 illustrates the second way people may "let go" (although in its context the verse does not refer to victims who let go). In the verse, *aphiēmi* means "to free or release someone from something," referring to being a wrongdoer and to the wrongdoing respectively; *aphiēmi* is then contrasted with *krateō*, which in its context means "to hold something in place," and so for it to remain unforgiven.

By choosing to use *aphiēmi* and *aphesis*, the writers of the Christian Scriptures imply that people face choices when they have been wronged. In relation to themselves, victims can choose to keep in mind the wrong and not let it go, or they can put it behind them and move on. In relation to wrongdoers, victims can let go, and so release, wrongdoers from their wrongs, or they can choose to continue to connect wrongdoers with the wrongdoing.

Aphiēmi and *aphesis* are also used when one person remits the debts of another. It is a word taken from the world of business and commerce. Metaphorically, the wrongs people did against one another or against God were sometimes thought of as being like debts that they (the wrongdoers) owed their victims. Victims could remit the "debt" that interpersonal wrongdoing gave rise to by forgiving the wrongdoers. We are familiar with the interpretation of forgiveness as being like the remission of debt: see the Lord's Prayer (Matt 6:12 and Luke 11:4) and the parable of the Unforgiving Servant (Matt 18:23–35).

Notice that, in relation to wrongdoers, when I have written about victims "letting go" of and forgiving wrongdoing, I have been careful not to say that victims release wrongdoers either from being guilty of wrongdoing, or from accountability for wrongdoing. Victims can do neither of these things; to suggest that they can is to arrogate to victims what some say is true of God but which is not true of human beings.

Charizomai

Less commonly used than *aphiēmi* and *aphesis* is a verb, *charizomai*. At its root, *charizomai* carries the idea of giving a gift or giving freely. It is a verb that Christians reformulated to refer to forgiveness. The verb can be used of canceling a debt (as in Luke 7:42–43) and by extension came to mean to show oneself gracious and generous by forgiving or pardoning a wrong. This verb brings out another idea about forgiving, the idea of doing a gracious act of kindness, when perhaps the opposite is due, and of giving someone a gift. We consider this verb further in chapter 9.

In Col 2:14, forgiveness, expressed in the preceding verse by the verb *charizomai*, is amplified by a phrase that means to "erase the record that stands against us." The word translated "erase" usually means "to wipe away" and can also mean "to remove so as to leave no trace," and even "obliterate." The word that is translated "record" means a "handwritten document," and almost always is a written record of debts. The important point for us is that in this verse, though in different language from Matt 6:12, Luke 11:4, and Matt 18:23–35, forgiveness is likened to the erasure of debt.

Apoluō

The last word, *apoluō*, is a common word in the Gospels and Acts, though it is used only once in the sense of "forgive," in Luke 6:37. This also appears to be a new meaning for the verb. At its root, the verb means to set free, to let go, divorce, send away, or release. It can also mean "to pardon," and that might be its meaning when Pilate debates whether to release Jesus from the sentence of death. (See Matt 27:15–26, for example.) This word points us to another aspect of what it means to forgive: the idea of offering release to someone from the wrong that he or she has done.

Summary

From the language used in the Christian Scriptures, we can say that:

- *Aphiēmi* and *aphesis* imply that a victim personally and relationally lets go of having been wronged;

- *Charizomai* suggests that a victim, even though having been wronged, gives a gift of undeserved favor to a wrongdoer; and

- *Apoluō* implies that a victim offers release from wrongdoing to a wrongdoer.

FORGIVENESS, SACRIFICE, AND THE DEATH OF JESUS

Interpersonal forgiveness usually involves victims relinquishing, and so (one might say) sacrificing, their rights against wrongdoers. As we shall see in chapter 13, some writers in the Christian Scriptures, such as the writer of Matthew, 1 John, and the writer to the Hebrews, understand Jesus's death to be sacrificial.[1] As a result, sacrificial acts, such as forgiving others, have been interpreted as reflecting or representing Jesus's sacrificial death, and in some way as integrated with it.[2]

However, we have to be careful not to make the sacrificial nature of Jesus's death the controlling idea for interpreting interpersonal forgiveness in the Christian Scriptures. This is because the interpretation of Jesus's death as sacrificial, widespread in popular theology though it is, is only one of several interpretations in the Christian Scriptures, and an interpretation probably only obvious in the Gospel of John, the letters of John, and in the letter to the Hebrews. Jesus's death is often understood and explained in other ways. For example, the death of Jesus is described as a "ransom" in Mark 10:45, and in Gal 2:20 Paul thinks of Jesus's death as an interchange[3] in which believers participate[4] by faith. Often understated is the fact that Luke explains the

1. It is now thought unlikely that in Rom 3:25 Paul regards Jesus's death as sacrificial: see Bailey, "Mercy Seat."

2. 2 Cor 4:10; Phil 3:10, 2 Cor 1:5, and Col 1:24.

3. Hooker, *From Adam*.

4. Sanders, *Paul*.

death of Jesus on the cross as bringing *aphesis* (letting go, release) of sin, and in consequence power to live a new way.

THE DRAWBACK OF METAPHORS

The writers of the Christian Scriptures use words that are metaphors to explain what they mean by interpersonal forgiveness. Metaphors are figures of speech that, because figures of speech, are not literally applicable. They are used to find points of comparison between apparently unlike things, and thereby help explain the subject of the comparison. If, when I am hungry, I say, "I could eat a horse!" I intend to say that I am so hungry I would like a large meal. I am not intending to say anything about my ability to eat, or that I would like to eat an entire horse. What we have to do to make sense of what I said is to find the relevant points of comparison between the "ground" (the subject to which attributes are ascribed—in this case, being hungry) and the "figure" (the object whose attributes are borrowed for the comparison—being able to eat a horse).

When it comes to forgiveness, the "ground" is forgiveness and the "figure" is words such as *aphiēmi* and *charizomai*. Understanding the metaphor is a literary exercise that depends on a creative response to analogy, and on its own is unlikely to help formulate a definition.

It is not surprising that the writers of the Christian Scriptures chose metaphors to explain interpersonal forgiveness. In the Judeo-Christian tradition, forgiveness is principally an action of God as a result of the atonement; interpersonal forgiveness is one of the appropriate, virtuous, ethical responses to the atonement that seeks to model the atonement, as best as human beings can. Language about God, including language about God's forgiveness, can only be figurative and analogical. Indeed, it is hard to see how language about God can be explored apart from by more metaphor. Interpersonal forgiveness is a scion of divine forgiveness—not the same and not as richly textured, but nevertheless genealogically related—and so necessarily also described and explained by metaphor.

SUMMARY

We have established that we cannot definitively define forgiveness but we can try to understand forgiveness by interpreting the metaphors that are used to explain it. Put simply, we can say that forgiveness, when used in the Christian Scriptures, is about letting go, about giving a gift of undeserved favor to a wrongdoer, and about offering and experiencing release from wrongdoing. These metaphors have to do with the way victims release wrongdoers from the wrongs they have done and the way victims release themselves from being victims of the wrongdoing. Explanations of the death of Jesus may also help inform what we understand interpersonal forgiveness to be.

QUESTIONS

1. With which vocabulary do the Christian Scriptures explain forgiveness?

2. What are some of the ways to explain interpersonal forgiveness?

Chapter 4

LIVING THE METAPHORS
OF FORGIVENESS

AFTER HAVING BEEN WRONGED, it is psychologically important to engage with the fact of being a victim; it is also important to move on, even if a wrongdoer does not repent. If one does not move on, one may remain a victim. It is psychologically unhelpful to remain trapped in victimhood. So what can one do to move on? In other words, how can one seek to become a forgiver and so live the metaphors of forgiveness?

FORGIVENESS AS A PROCESS

Psychological therapists talk about the stages of moving on from being a "victim," to being a "survivor," and finally to being a "thriver." Being a thriver requires engaging with having been wronged, growing through the experience of suffering, and integrating it into mature and balanced psychological health. The result, from a psychological view, will be release from being a victim. In fact, being a thriver involves more than surviving being a victim; it means moving on in a way so that one becomes a psychologically stronger, healthier person, and perhaps even a better person for having been wronged.

Because God's forgiveness is alluded to in terms that we might call "punctiliar" (that is, given at a point in time and apparently without antecedent reflection and preparation), we tend to understate the preparation that we need to make and undergo in order to be able to forgive. Expressing interpersonal forgiveness is, of course, punctiliar, since it happens at a point in time; however, getting to that point involves a process of preparation that can be psychological, spiritual, and social. For many people, this involves an inner journey of self-discovery that identifies different levels of hurt and suffering that have to be addressed before they are able to offer robust forgiveness.[1] The parable of the Prodigal Son (Luke 15:11–32) illustrates this point. By the time the son returned home, his father was ready to offer forgiveness, presumably having had time to prepare, and the son was ready to receive forgiveness, because (as we know from the parable) he too had had time to prepare.

Practically speaking, what do people typically address in order to become ready to forgive? Religious traditions may have suggestions that are germane to their own traditions. I propose to look at the question by focusing on three different aspects of human self-expression that are the subject of cognitive behavior therapy: thoughts, feelings (affect), and behavior. If we want to forgive, we may first have to address each of these three aspects of our personhood. Psychological therapists say that, of thoughts, feelings, and behavior, feelings are the hardest to change. They suggest that there is a link from thoughts to feelings, and that as people modify pathological patterns of thought their feelings will gradually change, and as their feelings and their

1. Among modern philosophers, Holmgren recognizes that forgiveness is a process: *Forgiveness*, 67.

thoughts change, so they will be empowered to change their behavior.

Behavior

Behavior is about making conscious choices about what to do or what not to do. Forgiving behavior can be recognized by the absence of actions that are vengeful or retributive, for example. In 1718, Bishop Joseph Butler, an English philosopher-Bishop, said in a sermon that in order to forgive, people must "forswear," that is, (in more modern language), forgo, resentment.[2] At their most simple, both "forswear" and "forgo" mean, "to relinquish." In other words, to forgive means to relinquish resentment. A modern example of such an approach to forgiveness is in an autobiographical movie *Beyond Forgiving* (2013) that features Ginn Fourie and Letlapa Mphahlele,[3] Ginn Fourie describes forgiveness as "a conscious and principled decision to give up [one's] justifiable right to revenge." Changing one's behavior, such as by forgoing resentment, is not a straightforward process, and may take time, even with support from psychological therapy. One must not be naïve about how difficult and lengthy the process may be.

Thoughts

Psychological therapists generally hold that people are not necessarily responsible for their thoughts. A thought is simply a thought, and nothing more. However, people are responsible for feeding unhelpful thoughts in unhelpful

2. *Sermons*, IX.

3. Letlapa Mphahele is former Director of Operations of the Azanian People's Liberation Army (APLA), the military wing of the Pan Africanist Congress (PAC). He gave an order in 1993 that led to the murder of Ginn Fourie's daughter, Lyndi, in what is known as "The Heidelberg Tavern Massacre" in Cape Town, South Africa.

ways. In contrast, the ethics of the Gospels are less nuanced, and tend not to distinguish between what people think and what people do. Generally, the Gospels assume that people can be as much culpable for their thoughts as for their actions (see Matt 5:21–30, for example). Certainly it is psychologically and theologically astute to recognize that actions spring from thoughts. Thoughts, however, are neutral; what matters is what people do as a result of their thoughts, and not simply the thoughts themselves.

How does one change one's thoughts if they are unforgiving? One can challenge one's thoughts, sometimes with the help of psychological therapy, by learning to manage one's negative thoughts. For example, one can choose to introduce new positive thoughts or choose not to ruminate on negative thoughts. Such actions are not a "cure" for negative thoughts, in the sense that the actions do not make the thoughts go away entirely, but they can have the effect not only of not feeding negative patterns of thought but also of causing them to atrophy so that they become insignificant. Through new patterns of thought and by investing in the richness of the opportunities they bring, one may find that former, unhelpful patterns of thought no longer have the power over our minds they once had.

There are unhelpful ways to change one's thoughts. For example, some people seem to think that in order to forgive, one must somehow stop regarding what W, a wrongdoer, did as wrong, in order to cease to feel resentment, and so to become able to forgive. What they tend to do, in my observation, is to understate to themselves W's wrongdoing or even to ignore it, thereby trying to make themselves think that they are doing what is necessary for the greater good of forgiving W. In other words, they believe that if they have a choice of either being robust about W's wrongdoing or forgiving W, it is better to opt for forgiving W and downplaying W's wrongdoing and its impact on them.

One does not have to make oneself believe what one knows is not right, or compromise one's integrity, in order to forgive. Forgiveness keeps in balance the fact that W has wronged V, a victim, without V also being inappropriately angry, or bitter, or vengeful. A principled, thoughtful response that insists that W did wrong does not preclude V from also being able to forgive W. Such a response balances V's integrity with the Christian injunctions to love one's enemies, not to be vengeful, and to forgive those who do wrong. An ethical framework that celebrates forgoing all resentment as always virtuous is, I suggest, undesirable and even misguided.

Feelings

Lastly, and most complexly, we turn to forgiving feelings. In Butler's view, forgiveness presupposes that people forgo "resentment" toward those who have wronged them. In the sense that Butler means it and according to the *Oxford English Dictionary*, resentment is a "sense of grievance; an indignant sense of injury or insult received or perceived; (a feeling of) ill will, bitterness, or anger against a person or thing." Thus, by "resentment" Butler is referring to feelings, and perhaps he also includes what people think.

Resentment is not always entirely negative. Butler recognizes that resentment can be well directed if it is "conducive to the end for which it was given us."[4] As the definition of resentment makes clear, resentment encompasses a range of responses, some of which may be appropriate and apposite. An example of the latter sort of resentment can

---

4. *Sermons*, IX.8; see Brudholm, *Resentment*, and Bash, *Ethics*, 47–51.

be what a person feels as a principled response to wrongdoing, and can be without bitterness or vengeful feelings and thoughts. Such resentment does not preclude someone from forgiving a wrongdoer. Not allowing oneself to be resentful can lead to psychological, and even physical, ill health. Immanuel Kant cruelly (but correctly, in my view) wrote in another context of those who are servile, "One who makes himself a worm cannot complain afterwards if people step on him."[5] In contrast, resentment that is characterized by ill will and bitterness does prevent a person from offering forgiveness to a wrongdoer.

One senses that Paul is aware of the difference between the two types of resentment because, on the one hand, he urges Christians to "put away all bitterness, wrath, and anger" (Eph 4:31), after having urged the same people, earlier in the same paragraph, to "be angry, and do not sin" (Eph 4:26). There is not a contradiction between the two passages if one draws the distinction between the two types of resentment that I describe above.

I do not think that all unhelpful resentment must be absent for forgiveness to take place; it is possible to forgive while retaining a modicum of unhelpful resentment. We have to be realistic about the fact that even the most forgiving of victims is rarely ever entirely without unhelpful resentment. Receiving a wrongdoer's contrition and remorse can, however, accelerate the final stages of healing from such resentment.

The challenge of getting ready to forgive is to move from resentment that is unhelpful to resentment that is appropriately focused and continues to hold W to account, without bitterness and vengeful feelings. Two independent, convergent processes usually need to be at work for V to forgive, and for both V and W to experience the regenerative

5. Kant, *Metaphysics*, 559.

and renewing power of forgiveness. The first is that V needs to find ways of causing the resentment V feels to become principled and appropriate. Second, W needs to demonstrate contrition and remorse. Contrition and remorse affirm that V's response to the wrongdoing is not perverse, indicate that W shares V's view about the wrongdoing, and can be the catalyst for further healing for V.

FORGIVENESS INTERVENTIONS

Some psychological therapists who practice cognitive behavior therapy have developed a pattern of therapy called "Forgiveness Interventions," which is designed to help people to forgive and to move on from what can be the destructive effects of un-forgiveness. (See, e.g., the work of the International Forgiveness Institute that helps disseminate the research findings of R. D. Enright and the Human Development Study Group at the University of Wisconsin–Madison.) Though I have some doubts about the theoretical basis of the therapy,[6] the effect of the interventions can be helpful for those whose psychological health is adversely affected by un-forgiveness.

UNILATERAL FORGIVENESS
AND SELF-FORGIVENESS

Forgiveness has to do with the restoration of relationships. As one would therefore expect, interpersonal forgiveness is typically bilateral, involving both wrongdoer and victim exploring what went wrong between them and seeking to put right their differences. However, sometimes it can be helpful for a victim to offer forgiveness before a wrongdoer

6. Bash, *Ethics*, 36–56, and Garrard and McNaughton, *Forgiveness*, 63–82.

has acknowledged he or she has done wrong. The effect of the offer can be a catalyst for bringing the wrongdoer to repentance and for restoring the wrongdoer to the victim. Even in this situation, forgiveness becomes bilateral.

When one wants to forgive but cannot (e.g., because the wrongdoer is not known or if the wrongdoer denies having done wrong), moving on in the way I have described can be of great personal benefit to a victim. It may involve a form of forgiveness that, though no more than in the mind of the victim, is offered to a wrongdoer and not necessarily known about or received by the wrongdoer. This sort of forgiveness is sometimes called "unilateral forgiveness." It does not bring about a restored relationship. Neither is it forgiveness as the Christian Scriptures understand it, since the restoration of ruptured relationships is not within its scope. Nevertheless, it is a form of forgiveness, though muted and limited, and can be necessary for the psychological health of the victim. For similar reasons and in similar circumstances, I believe it is possible for a repentant wrongdoer to "self-forgive" if the victim cannot be identified or if the victim will not offer forgiveness.[7]

QUESTIONS

1. To what extent is forgiveness a process?

2. Describe forgiveness in terms of thoughts, behavior, and feelings.

3. What is self-forgiveness? When might one self-forgive? Why is self-forgiveness less richly textured than bilateral forgiveness?

7. Bash, *Ethics*, 13–18.

Chapter 5

WHAT HAPPENS WHEN PEOPLE FORGIVE?

In the previous two chapters, we have seen that in the Christian Scriptures forgiveness carries with it the idea of personally and relationally letting go of having been wronged (*aphiēmi* and *aphesis*), of giving a gift of undeserved favor to a wrongdoer (*charizomai*), and of offering release from wrongdoing to the wrongdoer (*apoluō*). Forgiveness can be a sacrificial act, as a result of which victims give up their rights against wrongdoers. We have also seen that forgiveness can sometimes only be offered after a process of psychological and spiritual maturation. In this chapter, we explore some further aspects of what happens when people forgive.

FORGIVENESS AS A RESPONSE TO WRONGDOING

In the Hebrew Scriptures (as we have seen) and in the Christian Scriptures, God forgives sins, that is, wrongs against God in contravention of God's law. Interpersonal wrongs are not "sins" in the same sense, and the writers of the Christian Scriptures recognize this. For example, Matthew avoids the issue by choosing words about debt, which we have seen is a metaphor for sin, to describe what God and human beings each forgive (Matt 6:12). In contrast, in a parallel passage, Luke uses different words for what God forgives and for what human beings forgive (Luke 11: 4). He says that God forgives "sins" but people forgive "debtors." However, the distinction between the subject of God's forgiveness and the subject of interpersonal forgiveness may not be significant in this respect: divine forgiveness and interpersonal forgiveness are each a response to wrongdoing.

What is wrongdoing, as people then understood it? They already knew that not keeping the Jewish law was a reason for seeking God's forgiveness. Jesus offered an obvious way to identify the subject matter of the Jewish law, which is in contrast to the 613 commandments which later teachers of the law identified. Rather more simply, Jesus summarized the law as the duty to love God and to love one's neighbor.

It is not always clear, of course, how to love one's neighbor, because to love one's neighbor is do something that is situational and contingent. Thus, it was loving for the Good Samaritan to break his journey and care for a man who had been beaten up and left half dead (Luke 10:29–37); it might not be loving for a person running past the injured man to stop and tend him if the effect would be stop her from getting help to rescue her children and elderly relatives trapped in a burning house. In effect, what Jesus did was to restate the law from being understood as deontological (rule keeping) to being understood as teleological (evaluating the consequences of an act, rather than the act itself).

Of course, it was known that not loving one's neighbor was a sin against God, for which one should seek God's forgiveness. Jesus went further and clarified what was already implicit in Jewish thought, though not clearly appreciated:

not loving one's neighbor is also a wrong against one's neighbor, for which one should seek one's neighbor's forgiveness. Thus, one effect of restating the law is that not only God but also one's neighbor could be a forgiver. Another effect is to make the subject matter of forgiveness whatever is not loving. These are both astonishingly far-reaching developments in Jewish ethics and jurisprudence. We have lost sight of how radical they are, because we are familiar with them.

FORGIVENESS AND REPENTANCE

Both the Hebrew Scriptures and the Christian Scriptures presuppose that repentance is the starting point for forgiveness. Contrary to this view, it is sometimes said that on the cross, Jesus forgave those who crucified him. Luke 23:34 ("Father, forgive them, for they do not know what they are doing") is usually quoted in support at this point. Some suggest that, as he was dying, Jesus offered and gave forgiveness at enormous personal cost. They say that he forgave people who neither asked for nor sought his forgiveness. People add that Jesus's example of apparently unconditional forgiveness on the cross is the true pattern of forgiveness, and it is the pattern to which human beings should aspire. The same pattern of apparently unconditional forgiveness is also seen in Acts 7:60 where Stephen, the first Christian martyr, as he lay dying, prayed for those who were stoning him and said, "Lord, do not hold this sin against them." The implication of these observations about Jesus and Stephen is that a truly Christo-centric, cruciform[1] approach to

---

1. Michael Gorman uses this term in *Cruciformity*. By this, Gorman means that there is to be correspondence between the way a believer lives and the model of living and dying that Jesus demonstrated on the cross.

forgiveness means that people should always forgive even the unrepentant, as an undeserved gift of love and grace.

The suggestion that Jesus forgave his unrepentant killers is, in my view, a mistake. Jesus did not forgive those who were putting him to death, but prayed that *God* would not hold their sin against them. In other words, what he said does not amount to forgiveness of unrepentant people. Rather, it is Jesus's prayer, asking God to forgive those who had wronged him. For although his killers did know what they were doing (in the sense that they knew they were putting to death a man), they did not know or understand fully the implications of their actions.

However, we should not overlook the fact that by his words Jesus modeled an extraordinary measure of love, mercy, and prayerfulness for his enemies. He was also without any aspect of vengefulness. This observation points to the way to interpret the cross when it comes to interpersonal forgiveness: the cross exemplifies behavior that eschews revenge, and models seeking the best for one's enemies through love, mercy, and prayer.

Similar observations are true of Acts 7:60. Stephen did not say words of forgiveness to those who were stoning him for blasphemy. Rather, he prayed that God would not hold against his killers their unintended sin. The sin of Stephen's killers was unintended in this sense: they did not know that what Stephen had said was true. If, as with Saul of Tarsus, they came to understand that they had killed an innocent man because he had been telling the truth, the possibility of divine forgiveness would be available to them (see Lev 5:17–19). Luke, who probably wrote both Acts and the Gospel of Luke, highlights that Stephen modeled the same spirit of love, mercy, and prayer as Jesus, and, also like Jesus, was without vengeance in his response to his killers.

More generally, some people think that the ideal form of forgiveness is to forgive the unrepentant.[2] I do recognize that offering forgiveness to an unrepentant wrongdoer may be a trigger for helping the wrongdoer to reflect on what he or she has done and which may lead to the wrongdoer repenting. However, there are many difficulties with the view that it is generally virtuous to forgive the unrepentant. For example, the effect of forgiving an unrepentant wrongdoer may be to leave the wrongdoer free to escape accountability as a personally responsible agent; it may also deny the wrongdoer both the incentive and the opportunity to right the wrong. The wrongdoer will not learn from former mistakes, and so may continue to harm others. Moreover, and perhaps surprisingly, to urge a victim to offer forgiveness freely to a wrongdoer when the wrongdoer is unrepentant is to lay on the victim a greater obligation than appears to be on God, who seems to forgive only the repentant who seek, or who see the need for, forgiveness. Perhaps most persuasive of all is the scenario, which I have personally observed of victims, eager to forgive wrongdoers who do not know that they have done wrong (and who, even if they did know, would not be concerned), saying they forgive those who have wronged them. In such circumstances, wrongdoers can be bewildered, even amused, at the offer of forgiveness, for there is no meeting of minds or of values about the acts or omissions in question.

FORGIVENESS, REVENGE, AND RETRIBUTION

Not taking revenge or not exacting retribution are synonymous with what Butler means by "forswearing resentment."

2. For a philosophical defense of the view that forgiveness does not necessarily have to be dependent on repentance, see Garrard and McNaughton, *Forgiveness*, 117–19.

So when a victim forgives a wrongdoer by letting go of wrongdoing and offering release from the wrongdoing, we generally assume that a victim will not also choose to take revenge or to exact retribution.

In contemporary Western society, revenge and retribution, when exacted by individuals, are usually regarded as unacceptable;[3] they are also sometimes unlawful. If you break my window, I may not break yours. It is, however, easy to assume that revenge and retribution are always undesirable. If you wrong me, I may decide no longer to invite you to my home for dinner, to send you a birthday card and present, or to return your phone calls. Such actions might be called "the socially acceptable face of revenge and retribution," and in some situations they are among the appropriate ways to respond to having been wronged.

Sometimes, revenge and retribution are undertaken through judicial proceedings on behalf of individuals who have been wronged. In light of this, the question is asked whether one can choose to initiate proceedings against an individual at the same time as intending to forgive that individual. In 1 Cor 6:1–8, Paul takes the view that disputes between church members should be settled internally in the church, rather than publicly, in the courts. His argument is not based on the incongruity of pursuing legal proceedings while holding to an ethic of forgiveness. Rather, it is based on the incongruity of Christians being judges at the *eschaton* (the end of the world and of time) but not being able to resolve their own internal differences.

In my view, it is not possible to initiate legal proceedings and still to intend to forgive, because legal proceedings are institutionalized forms of taking revenge or exacting retribution. To put it colloquially, one "cannot have it both ways"; that is, one cannot implicitly choose not to take

3. Compare Murphy, *Getting Even*, 17.

revenge or to exact retribution as part of what it means to forgive, while at the same time pursuing revenge and retribution through the courts or legal system.

THE "PROVISIONALITY" OF FORGIVENESS

We also tend to think that forgiving and being forgiven, once made, are final and irrevocable. The idea of forgiveness as "performative utterance" (making a statement that is a constitutive part of the act of forgiving and that functions as a promise) has added to this idea.[4]

Forgiveness is sometimes irreversible, and intended always to be so, whatever in the future may arise. An example is from Eric Lomax's autobiography, *The Railway Man* (1996) (now a movie, made in 2013, with the same title). Lomax had spent close on half a century hating the man who had participated in his torture in a Japanese prisoner-of-war-camp in the Second World War. Through an extraordinary set of circumstances that began in 1989, Lomax was able to trace the man who had been the translator during the torture, Nagase Takashi. With the help of psychological therapy, careful reflection, and as a result of meeting Nagase, Lomax realized "the hating has to stop"[5] and was ready to forgive Nagase. In a private encounter in Tokyo, Lomax read out to Nagase a letter that expressed his forgiveness. The letter constituted an irrevocable and irreversible decision to forgive. Lomax wrote, "I read my short letter out to him, stopping and checking that he understood each paragraph. . . . I told him that while I could not forget what happened . . . , I assured him of my total forgiveness."[6]

4. Haber, *Forgiveness*.
5. Lomax, *Railway Man*, 276.
6. Ibid., 275.

However, the outcome of forgiveness is not always as clear-cut as this. Consider, for example, the following real-life example. A friend suffered from the effects of negligent surgery and was unable to bear children as a result. In her thirties, she grieved as her friends carried and gave birth to children. My friend eventually felt able to forgive the surgeon for his foolishness and negligence. However, in later life, when her friends became grandparents, she found that her anger and resentment returned, as she realized that she would not be a grandparent. Whereas once she thought she had forgiven and been able to put the past behind her, new circumstances arose that re-opened the wound she still carried and meant that my friend had to start the work of forgiveness again.

It is surely foolish to say "I forgive you" and assume that nothing in the future might arise that will re-open the wounds of the past or mean that one has to renew the work of forgiving. One might have been able to forgive what one knows about in relation to a wrong, but if one discovers new information that renders the basis of the forgiveness doubtful, the forgiveness can become un-forgiveness.

Additionally, many of us will have seen someone, or returned to a place, or heard a piece of music that brings back memories about a former unpleasant experience. If that experience relates to having been wronged, one might find that one needs to re-engage with having to forgive, or realize that one has more to forgive. People may sometimes be wrong if, after an act of forgiveness, they think they have completed all the work of forgiving that may arise in relation to the wrong.

I suggest, therefore, that forgiveness can best be thought of as reversible and revocable, though it should not be offered with this possibility in mind. The parable of the Unforgiving

Servant in Matt 18:23–35 seems to presuppose that forgiveness may be revoked if the circumstances merit it.

This observation discloses a paradox about forgiveness, namely, that it is both irrevocable and revocable at the same time. On the one hand, it is no good saying, "I forgive you for the wrong you have done to me, but I may, if I wish, revoke the forgiveness," because that would leave the wrongdoer as if "on parole" and no more than temporarily forgiven until the forgiver may change his or her mind. On the other hand, one has to be realistic and recognize that sometimes the work that led to the act of forgiving is in fact incomplete or unravels, and what formerly was forgiveness is no longer so. One can have more forgiving to do, even when we thought we had forgiven all that there is to forgive.

Is God's forgiveness revocable? Heb 10:18 (with Heb 10:14) suggest that God's forgiveness of sins is given once and is irrevocable, whereas Heb 6:4–6, 10:26–31 suggest the opposite. As we shall see, some sayings of Jesus in the Gospels indicate that divine forgiveness can be lost if people are unforgiving toward others. On balance, and as we shall see later in this book, for the most part, the Christian Scriptures indicate that people can do things that may result in the loss of divine forgiveness.

By analogy, does this suggest that interpersonal forgiveness can also be lost?

I observe in chapter 8 that divine forgiveness and interpersonal forgiveness, though similar in some respects, also have important differences. It is a mistake to assume that because divine forgiveness can be lost, so interpersonal forgiveness can also be lost. However, our analysis of interpersonal behavior and the brief reference to Matt 18:23–35 above indicates that people can sometimes find themselves out of forgiving relationships with those who had formerly forgiven them. That one can lose interpersonal forgiveness and/or divine forgiveness is not, I suggest, mere coincidence of aspects of otherwise discrete behaviors, but a risk that goes with being forgiven, whether by another human being or by God.

SUMMARY

Forgiveness in the Christian Scriptures is a response to wrongdoing and is almost always preceded by the wrongdoer's repentance. Forgiveness eschews revenge and retribution. Though it is not offered this way, forgiveness is provisional, in the sense that it may be revoked or reversed.

QUESTIONS

1. What are the characteristic features of a forgiving response to wrongdoing?

2. Which types of responses to wrongdoing can undermine or negate an intention to forgive?

3. What can be said for and against the view that a victim may forgive a wrongdoer who has been prosecuted for wrongdoing?

4. Do you agree that forgiveness is typically "provisional"? Why or why not?

Chapter 6

CONTEMPORARY FORGIVENESS

To WHAT EXTENT IS the framework of forgiveness in the Christian Scriptures that I have been identifying congruent with contemporary understandings of forgiveness? In the following pages, I identify five, typical characteristics of forgiveness as forgiveness is generally recognized in Western society today. I begin first with some reflections on wrongdoing, the subject matter of forgiveness.

WRONGDOING

Some of the time, what is "wrongdoing" is easy to identify. Forgiveness "works" well in a world of clear moral values; it is considerably more problematic where there is disagreement about the framework of ethical norms that is to be followed. It does not work at all if a victim or wrongdoer denies that there is anything to forgive. For example, it can be difficult for those who believe they are victims of wrongdoing to encounter wrongdoers who deny that they (the wrongdoers) have done wrong. It can be equally difficult for wrongdoers who know they have done wrong to be denied the opportunity of being forgiven if they seek forgiveness, when their victims deny that they (the victims) are victims or that there is anything to forgive.

I came across the following example of incongruent moral values in a pastoral situation that a colleague faced.[1] John left his wife, Kate, and their three young children, because, he said, he was homosexual. John later disclosed that he was with Larry, a new partner, with whom he had had a secret relationship for some years. Shortly after the breakup of the marriage and before Kate knew of Larry's existence, Kate wanted to forgive John for breaking the promises he had made when they married and for the fact that he had not been truthful about his sexuality. John denied there was anything to forgive because (he said) his marriage promises were based on an out-of-date view of marriage, and of heterosexual marriage at that. When Kate later discovered that John had a new partner, Larry, she took away her and John's children and hid them from him. She denied that she was doing wrong because, she said, she was "protecting the children" from John and Larry, and their "influence on impressionable minors." In both situations (John having reneged on his marriage promises, and Kate having hidden the children of the marriage from John) there was an impasse, with the supposed victims and supposed wrongdoers not in agreement about whether anything had taken place that was wrong and so forgivable.

There are situations that arise where people of integrity disagree whether there has been wrongdoing, and so disagree about whether there is anything to forgive. In such situations, it seems to me to be both truthful and loving to acknowledge the viewpoint of the other and to respond accordingly. I can see nothing wrong with saying to a supposed victim, "I know that you think my actions are wrong

1. I have changed the names of the people concerned in the example.

51

and I am sorry that they have caused you hurt." (Notice that I wrote, "I am sorry *that*." In my view, to be sorry "if" offers only a hypothetical apology, and does not concede the point in dispute; to be sorry "that" concedes the point, and amounts to a real apology.) I also see nothing wrong with saying to a supposed wrongdoer, "I know you want me to forgive you for the wrong you think you have done to me; I want to assure you that I do not consider you have done wrong to me or that I have been hurt by your actions."

Also integral to forgiveness is the idea that wrongdoers, who recognize and acknowledge that they have done something that is wrong, make an appropriate response that demonstrates they know they have overstepped a boundary. Mere cognitive assent to having done wrong is not enough, as any parent knows when a child says "I am sorry" with the intent of no more than to avoid parental displeasure. As for adults, we have probably all heard what is sometimes called a "footballer's apology," that is, an apology that has clearly been drafted by a lawyer for a public figure (such as a footballer) usually for a crime or moral lapse, and which one suspects the person apologizing does not truly mean. Rather, what should characterize people who acknowledge that they have done wrong are remorse, contrition, honest engagement with the act (or omission) and its typical outward effects: repentance, and, when appropriate, reparation. Of course, one needs to keep a sense of balance about the degree and extent of the way people respond to their wrongdoing; what is needed is evidence of what seems to be a genuine and appropriate response to the wrong that has been done and the consequences that ensued.

As I was writing this chapter, I watched an online news broadcast about the public apology of Lou Vincent, a New Zealander cricketer, who admitted to attempting to "fix" cricket matches. The BBC news report about his apology states that "in [the first] 10 words [of the statement], [he] admits what he has done, how he has contravened and undermined his own sport by accepting money for match-fixing. Viewers are left in no doubt."[2] In the statement, Vincent says he wants to face up to what he has done "like a man and accept the consequences." The reporter described the statement as "unusually stark." To me as a viewer, with no specialist knowledge of cricket (despite being British!) the statement comes across as authentic and compelling, and as an honest attempt to tell the truth, and to face the truth and its consequences.

THE CHARACTERISTICS OF CONTEMPORARY FORGIVENESS

Scenario 1

Suppose W, a wrongdoer, defames V, a victim. The wrongdoing is actionable in the courts. Rather than go to court, V chooses to forgive W, because W and V are long-standing friends and because W is sorry about what she has done. By forgiving W, V implicitly declares (among other things) that W has wronged her and that she is setting aside the right to take legal proceedings against W for the wrongdoing. Legally, V can still sue W for the wrong (as her legal rights are unchanged); however, and as I have said in chapter 5, it is contrary to what is implicit in what it means to forgive if V pursues her legal rights against W.

Personally and relationally, what happens when V forgives W in this typical scenario? W regrets the wrong and wants a restored relationship with V. V wants a restored relationship with W. To help achieve this, V decides

2. Parkinson, "Lou Vincent."

to forgo her legal and other rights against W. Five elements are present in V's forgiveness: (i) a mutual recognition that W has *wronged* V, (ii) W's *repentance*, (iii) a mutual desire for a *restored relationship*, and (iv) V voluntarily *relinquishing her rights* against W. In this example, we also see that (v) V wishes to *release* W from the wrong. I suggest these five elements are typically present when a victim forgives a wrongdoer.

Scenario 2

In this scenario, W seriously assaults V. The wrongdoing is actionable in the courts. V recognizes that she has been wronged. W is deeply remorseful about the wrongdoing and tells V she wants to put right matters between herself and V. V also wants matters put right. However, the local police force decides to prosecute W for the crime. (Note that a third party is bringing proceedings, not V.) What is now of interest to us is whether, and if so when, V may forgive W if legal proceedings are taken against W.

We already know that W and V recognize that V has been wronged and that W is repentant; V is willing to release W from the wrong. Three of the five typical characteristics of forgiveness we identified above are present. If a third party begins legal proceedings in respect of the wrong, can the other two elements of forgiveness be present, that is, can we show that V and W both want a restored relationship, and can V voluntarily relinquish her rights against W? We consider the question from two viewpoints.

The first viewpoint is this. Suppose V believes that the relationship with W can be restored only if W has expiated her guilt through legal proceedings and by serving her sentence. V endorses the criminal prosecution and understands it to be part of the process that can bring about a restored relationship through forgiveness. If V offers "forgiveness" this way, it is doubtful that she is in fact offering forgiveness at all, because the offer appears to be calculative, a *quid pro quo* for punishment, set in the context of vengeance and retribution that are (in effect) carried out on behalf of V by the courts.

The second viewpoint is different. Suppose V regards court proceedings that have been initiated by a third party as being for the good of W, and perhaps for the good of society. Suppose also that V does not favor legal proceedings as the best way to resolve the wrong, and does not regard the likely sentence in a vengeful or retributive way. Imagine, too, that W agrees that the way to express remorse and repentance is to submit to a criminal prosecution and a sentence of punishment. Can we say in these circumstances that V and W have a mutual desire for a restored relationship? I think we can, if we remember two other things: first, that a third party, and not V, initiated the legal proceedings; second, that V is not motivated by vengeance or a desire for retribution. When all these factors are put together, it becomes obvious that both V and W have a desire for a restored relationship. In other words, we have another of the five elements of forgiveness that we identified above.

Can we now also say that the last element of forgiveness is present, namely that V has opted to relinquish her rights against W? (In this context, I am referring not only to legal rights, but also to opportunities freely to make and exercise choices.) One obvious right that V has is a right to discontinue her relationship with W because of the wrongdoing. I suggest that, since V chooses not to end the relationship with W because of the wrongdoing, she does give up rights. I am sure many who read this book will know someone who says of a wrongdoer something such as, "Because of what he did to me, I will never speak to or see him again." So long as V does not say or think something like this, but instead does what she can to relinquish impediments to rebuilding the relationship, we can legitimately say V has relinquished her rights against W. This is no more than another way of saying that V desires a restored relationship and, like W (who shows her hope for a restored relationship by repenting), responds appropriately to help bring about that restoration.

We conclude then that it can be possible for V to forgive W, even if legal proceedings have been instituted against W for the wrongdoing.

Scenario 3

What happens if we take out of the discussion the question of W having committed a wrong the courts have jurisdiction to deal with? (This is much more typical of situations in which questions of forgiveness arise.) For example, suppose W tells a significant untruth to V to create dissension among a group of friends. W realizes the folly of what she has done, becomes deeply remorseful, and seeks to put right what she has done. V wants to forgive W for the wrong and rebuild their relationship. Four of the five typical characteristics of forgiveness that we have identified are obviously present if V is to forgive W: a wrong, W's repentance, the mutual desire of W and V for a restored relationship, and V's desires to release W from the wrong. However, it is not so obvious in this case what V relinquishes. It might be her right to respond to W in the form of "the socially acceptable face of revenge and retribution" that I referred to earlier. It might also be other impediments to rebuilding the relationship. Whichever it may be, we can see that V can indeed relinquish her rights against W.

Interpretation

We have seen that forgiveness in today's Western world typically has five elements. All five elements express a mutual desire for a restored relationship. In other words, forgiveness can take place when both parties are committed to restoring an estranged relationship. For a wrongdoer, this is typically evidenced by contrition, repentance, and perhaps even reparation. For a victim, this is evidenced by the victim voluntarily surrendering the right to what might impede the restoration of the relationship and releasing the wrongdoer from the wrongs.

What is significant, I suggest, is that none of these elements is inconsistent with forgiveness in the Christian Scriptures. An analysis of forgiveness in relation to realistic contemporary examples may use different language from the Christian Scriptures. Both, however, focus on a single, overarching process: the restoration of a damaged or broken relationship.

QUESTIONS

1. What are the contemporary features of a forgiving response to wrongdoing?

2. To what extent are the contemporary features of a forgiving response to wrongdoing similar to and different from the way the Christian Scriptures outline a forgiving response to wrongdoing?

Chapter 7

RECONCILIATION, RESTORATION, AND FORGIVENESS

In a book on forgiveness, why have I included a chapter on reconciliation? I suggest for at least two reasons.

The first is that one of the outcomes of forgiveness is the restoration of damaged or broken relationships, which may mean that the parties, if restored, are back to where they were before the wrongdoing occurred and so reconciled. (The situation the parties were in before the wrongdoing occurred is sometimes called "the *status quo ante*.")

However, not all people who are restored are also reconciled. For example, if a wrongdoer has been violent toward a victim, it might not be appropriate for the victim to return to a situation with the wrongdoer where the violence could recur. It is better for the victim and the wrongdoer, even if they have forgiven one another, to go their separate ways and have no further contact. They now have a restored, but diminished, relationship and the *status quo ante* will not have been reestablished.

If there is reconciliation, even to say that the *status quo ante* will have been reestablished can be an oversimplification, because a former relationship may not only have been reestablished but also even enhanced. This may be because the parties have talked about their differences and conflicts, and as a result have put right the particular instance of what went wrong and repaired some underlying dysfunctional elements of their relationship. The result is that what they now have is better than what they enjoyed before.

The second reason for writing a chapter on reconciliation in a book on forgiveness is that people usually think that reconciliation is the end-point of a process that necessarily includes forgiveness, or something akin to it. (That is why reconciliation is sometimes referred to as "the teleology of forgiveness.") This may sometimes be right; it is worth noting, however, that if a wrongdoer, W, and a victim, V, restore their relationship after wrongdoing, there may be a measure of restoration, but not necessarily also forgiveness. Suppose, for example, that W and V are work colleagues, engaged in a joint project, and W wrongs V but denies that what he did is wrong; in such a situation, there probably cannot be forgiveness because W denies there is anything to be forgiven. However, if W and V still need to continue to work together, they may decide on a way to get along with each other, even though the issue between them remains unresolved. They are restored so they can work together, but no more than that.

In the Christian Scriptures, forgiveness and reconciliation are not explicitly paired. For example, in Rom 5:6–11, Paul interprets the death of Jesus on the cross as "justifying" and so "saving" sinners from God's wrath (v. 9). In consequence, sinners are "reconciled" to God (vv. 10–11). Nothing is said about forgiveness, though as we shall see in chapter 14, what Paul means by "justification" overlaps with forgiveness. Similarly, in 2 Cor 5:18–20, Paul explains that

God has reconciled men and women to himself through Christ, by not counting their sins against them. In this passage Paul does not also write of forgiveness. In verse 21 Paul talks of those "in Christ" having "the righteousness of God." By using language related to righteousness (in Greek "justification" and "righteousness" are etymologically related), Paul introduces what also overlaps with forgiveness.

The significance of what I am saying is this: in the Christian Scriptures there is a variety of metaphors and models to explain the atonement. None of the metaphors and models singly exhausts what is meant by the atonement; when all the passages are read compositely, they go toward depicting and describing the atonement, with each explicating the others. The result is that, although sometimes there appears to be no immediately obvious link between justification, forgiveness, and reconciliation, they are "genealogically" related, as they all refer to the atonement, and they all have restored relationships as their goal.

PERSONAL AND COMMUNAL RELATIONSHIPS

Every reference to interpersonal forgiveness in the Synoptic Gospels is, as we shall see, a reference to one-to-one relationships, and not to communities or groups. The same is true in the remainder of the Christian Scriptures, except the odd and obscure verses in 2 Cor 2 (which we explore in chapter 9). This is surprising, given that in the ancient world personal identity was principally understood in collective and corporate terms. One would have expected forgiveness in the Christian Scriptures to be as much a collective virtue as a personal virtue. However, it is not, although it is true that individual relationships were understood and experienced in the context of community life.

Perhaps the writers of the Christian Scriptures were generally wise to think of forgiveness as primarily interpersonal, and not as communal or collective. There are powerful, logical reasons why groups cannot forgive and be forgiven. I have set these out at length elsewhere.[1] Two obvious points: at best groups have only a legal, not ontological, identity, and that since group decisions taken by group representatives may not represent the views of the entire group, group representatives do not necessarily speak for everyone in the group.

Despite the analytical difficulties of what we mean by groups forgiving and being forgiven, groups can sometimes take a collective decision to forgive. There are, of course, excellent pragmatic reasons why groups should collectively express contrition for past wrongdoing and separate themselves from past foolishness. Such actions can lead to restored relationships, with the wronged group or individuals agreeing that the offending group has renounced its former wrongdoing.

Rather less problematic is the idea that groups can take steps to be reconciled. For example, estranged groups can set up mechanisms to begin dialog and engagement. These can lead to restored relationships, as a result of which past wrongdoing can become regarded as dealt with, and its place in the collective memory of the wronged community set aside. Reconciliation seen this way is a process that does not presuppose forgiveness, may take place over a lengthy period, and is usually measured in incremental steps.

In contrast with interpersonal forgiveness, reconciliation in the Christian Scriptures is primarily understood in collective, not individual, terms. For example, the context of Rom 5 and 2 Cor 5 (which we referred to above) slides between primarily corporate to sometimes individual. In

1. Bash, *Ethics*, 111–40.

Eph 2:11–22, the cross is understood as being the mechanism for reconciling to God two ethnic groups (Jews and Gentiles) of which one, the Gentiles, has previously been estranged from the Jewish covenant of faith (2:16). The logical next step in Paul's thinking is that since God has reconciled Jew and Gentile to God on an equal basis, Jew and Gentile are to live together, side by side, in love and peace. The letter to the Ephesians is in part written to promote that unity.

AN OBSERVATION

It is odd that the writers of the Christian Scriptures do not obviously link forgiveness and reconciliation, as they are both aspects of the atonement and both concern restored relationships. There are two reasons for this. I have already in part suggested the first, namely, that forgiveness and reconciliation are different facets of the atonement. At the time when the Christian Scriptures were being written, they were genealogically, but not intellectually, linked. The second reason is that the models of behavior that were drawn on to explain the atonement and its implications for human behavior come from different cultures and patterns of thought: divine forgiveness in the Hebrew Scriptures is the basis of the model for interpersonal forgiveness in the Christian Scriptures, and secular Greek thought the model for a theology of reconciliation.[2] It has been for later generations to recognize the obvious connections between the two models and to affirm that both models are important approaches to restoring relationships. For these reasons, in a book on forgiveness in the Christian Scriptures, such as this one, we cannot ignore the important relationship of forgiveness and reconciliation to one another.

2. Bash, "Spirituality."

QUESTIONS

1. How are forgiveness and reconciliation related?
2. Do you think groups can forgive and be forgiven? Why or why not?

Chapter 8

WHO CAN—AND MAY— FORGIVE WHOM?

IT MAY SEEM STRANGE to ask the question, "Who can— and may—forgive whom?" in a book on forgiveness. The question is important because in an essay published in 1975, Anne Minas argued that it was impossible for God to forgive. More recently, Jacques Derrida argued in a lecture published in 2001 that it is impossible for human beings to forgive. We consider in this chapter whether they are right and what the implications their views might have for a theology of forgiveness. We also consider who may broker forgiveness.

CAN GOD FORGIVE?

"Far from its being the case that divine nature makes its possessor especially prone to forgive," Anne Minas wrote, "such a nature makes forgiveness impossible."[1] Minas takes as her starting point the definition of forgiveness given in the *Oxford English Dictionary* and on that basis convincingly argues that it is impossible for God to forgive. She summarizes,

1. Minas, "God and Forgiveness," 138.

"Only a human being can forgive—a divine being cannot."[2] Her conclusion is that "we cannot without logical and/or moral absurdity say of a fully divine being that it forgives."[3]

Is Minas Right?

The flaw in Minas's argument lies in the essay's starting point. The description of forgiveness that Minas takes from the *Oxford English Dictionary* is theologically naïve, and is no more than a description of interpersonal forgiveness. In adopting the dictionary's description as her starting point, Minas assumes that the description applies to all types of forgiveness, including divine forgiveness. As we shall see, she is mistaken. What the essay shows, albeit unintentionally, is that divine forgiveness is different from forgiveness offered by human beings to each other. This seems unexceptional, since human beings, though made in the image of God, are not God.

The Relationship of Divine Forgiveness to Interpersonal Forgiveness

We saw in chapter 2 that in the Hebrew Scriptures divine forgiveness is a gift, the elective action and response of God to human entreaty. It is given to those who are remorseful, repentant, and who, when it is appropriate, offer reparation for what they have done. Sacrifices were sometimes offered for forgiveness (see, e.g., Lev 4 and 5, and Num 15), but in even these situations, the sacrifices are in nature another type of entreaty for forgiveness.

Broadly speaking, forgiveness described in this way has parallels with the forgiveness that human beings can offer. However, in other respects divine forgiveness is different from interpersonal (human) forgiveness. For example,

2. Ibid., 138.
3. Ibid., 150.

God can set aside human sin[4] and so choose to purify and cleanse.[5] God can remove sin and its effects by taking away the sin,[6] and God can choose not to remember sin.[7] Punishment can be avoided in these circumstances though, occasionally, it is transferred to another.[8] Other ways that forgiveness is described include God casting sin behind God's back (Isa 38:17) or into the depths of the sea (Mic 7:19), treading sin underfoot (Mic 7:19), removing it "as far as the east is from the west" (Ps 103:12), and removing and blotting it out (Neh 4:5).

Divine forgiveness described in these ways is not without difficulty, for it does not appear to be entirely self-consistent with other aspects of divine self-disclosure. For example, in whichever ways we look at the metaphors about divine forgiveness in the Hebrew Scriptures, it is impossible to "square the circle" and explain how a divine being can be regarded as just, while at the same time choosing to forget or overlook wrongs, remit punishment, make exceptions to rules, and reverse previous judgments. It is also hard to see how human wrongdoing constitutes wrong against God. If W, a wrongdoer, tells a lie to V, a victim, it is not obvious that W has wronged God and so opening up the possibility that God will forgive W. Perhaps the solution is that we should say that the moral code God gives is so closely allied to God's identity and being as to mean that a breach of the code is a wrong against God. In other words, God and the moral code are impossible to distinguish.

---

4. Heb 9:26.

5. Ps 51:2 and Jer 33:8. See also 1 John 1:9.

6. See, e.g., Exod 34:7, Lev 16:21–22, Ps 32:1–5 (in part quoted in Rom 4:7), Ps 85:3, Isa 27:9, Ezek 16:62–63, and Mic 7:18. From the Christian Scriptures, Rev 1:5 says that Jesus "frees" from sin.

7. Ps 25:6–7, Isa 43:25, and Jer 31:34.

8. 2 Sam 12:13–14; 24:10–17, 25.

Conclusion

Notwithstanding these apparent difficulties, the Hebrew Scriptures and the Christian Scriptures say that God does and can forgive. Human knowledge of God can only be analogical and metaphorical, that is, explained and understood in terms of what human beings are like. Since human beings forgive, to say that God forgives can be a meaningful statement, though it does not follow that God necessarily forgives in the same way that human beings do. Minas has unintentionally highlighted that this is so.

CAN HUMAN BEINGS FORGIVE ONE ANOTHER?

People have always from time to time forgiven one another, and it is only recently that the question has been asked whether human beings *can* forgive one another. The question is important, and needs to be explored, as the answer to the question will point to whether a theology of forgiveness is useful or relevant.

In the Christian Scriptures, interpersonal forgiveness is commended as virtuous. Despite the relative paucity of references to interpersonal forgiveness, forgiveness rightly has an important place in the way people think about the balance of emphasis in the Christian Scriptures. An example of the significance of forgiveness is in the Lord's Prayer (Matt 6:12 and Luke 11:4), where it is as much explicit that people should forgive the wrongs done against them, as it is explicit that God forgives human beings. We can go further: in the Christian Scriptures, divine forgiveness and human forgiveness are seen as dependent upon one another, thereby giving interpersonal forgiveness a central place in the way the Christian gospel is presented and explained, for talk of God's forgiveness necessarily leads to talk of interpersonal forgiveness. God's forgiveness and interpersonal forgiveness go together and, theologically, they cannot be separated.

In an essay published in 2001, Jacques Derrida argued that genuine interpersonal forgiveness is impossible. His argument presents a significant challenge to Judeo-Christian ethics and practice. If Derrida is right, a characteristic marker of Christian discipleship will be redundant. On what does he base his argument?

For Derrida, interpersonal forgiveness exists only as a theoretical possibility but not as a reality. He says that "genuine forgiveness must engage two singularities: the guilty and the victim. As soon as a third party intervenes, one can again speak of amnesty, reconciliation, reparation, etc., but certainly not of forgiveness in the strict sense."[9] Anything that mediates between a wrongdoer and a victim, including even language, compromises the purity of the forgiveness because, in Derrida's view, it has become conditional. To put it in theological language (which Derrida does not), forgiveness is like grace, a gift given unconditionally without reference to anyone or anything except the decision of the giver. Genuine interpersonal forgiveness is therefore impossible, according to Derrida, because it can never be given in a way that does not compromise its purity. Derrida calls this impasse an "aporia," by which he means that forgiveness is a paradox. He expresses the paradox this way: "forgiveness forgives only the unforgivable."[10]

Critique of Derrida

On his own terms, Derrida is right when he says "forgiveness forgives only the unforgivable," because language will always intervene to compromise the purity of Derridean

9. Derrida, *On Cosmopolitanism*, 42.
10. Ibid., 32.

forgiveness. However, I suggest that Derrida's initial starting point is flawed. Interpersonal forgiveness that is wholly unconditional and untainted by any element of duty, obligation, or self-interest, is characteristic of divine forgiveness as described in the Hebrew Scriptures. Derrida thereby makes a mistake that is the converse of Minas's: Minas analyzed divine forgiveness as if it were human forgiveness, and so found it wanting, whereas Derrida analyzed human forgiveness as if it were divine, and so also, not surprisingly, found it to be wanting. In both cases (that of Minas and Derrida), the error is terminological and implicitly circular.

It is worth adding that even if Derridean pure forgiveness were possible, such forgiveness would be flawed, for pure interpersonal forgiveness, far from being desirable but impossible, is on close examination absurd and so undesirable. The absurdity has been elegantly illustrated in a different context by Michael Lapsley, who asks, "If you steal my bicycle and I forgive you, who keeps the bicycle?"[11] If I believe that my forgiveness must be pure and unconditional, without first looking for your repentance or expecting restitution, there is no reason why you should not keep the bicycle. According to Derrida, there must not be any sort of connection between my forgiveness and your wrongdoing. Forgiveness delineated this way is clearly nonsensical, and not forgiveness at all in any generally construed sense of what the word "forgiveness" means.

"The Predicament of Irreversibility"

Although Derrida does not say this, forgiveness will be impossible if by "forgiveness" we mean that wrongdoer and victim put right the past. The reason is connected with an observation of Hannah Arendt. Arendt has coined the

11. Lapsley, *Redeeming*, 152.

phrase "the predicament of irreversibility."[12] By this she means that an act once done cannot be undone. (Arendt suggests that the predicament can be reversed; she may be right, though I doubt it.) At the most, forgiveness only undoes the relational violation that wrongdoing causes and not the wrong itself, even if that wrong is forgiven. So if V forgives W for lying to him, their relationship may be restored but the fact W lied to V at a certain point in time cannot be undone or reversed. The wrong has taken place and they cannot "put back the clock" and reverse time, and they cannot undo the fact of a misdeed having been committed. Neither can "guilt be erased, nor can even punishment undo a deed."[13] What can be restored is the rupture the relationship that the wrongdoing caused. But unlike in the movie *Back to the Future* (1985), we cannot go back into the past and put right mistakes that have been made. We have to be careful, therefore, not to claim too much for interpersonal forgiveness. It is impossible if we assume it can put right the past. It is not impossible if we recognize that it can help restore relationships.

Forgiveness as an Amalgam

Rather than apparently dismissing interpersonal forgiveness as impossible, which Derrida appears to do, I suggest that interpersonal forgiveness exists always in the form of an amalgam, in the context of relations between the victim and the wrongdoer. The amalgam will, to a greater or lesser extent, have some of the characteristics of "pure" forgiveness, and despite being an alloy, will often still be forgiveness.[14] "Pure" forgiveness, without elements of other forms

12. Arendt, *Human Condition*, 237.
13. Nietzsche, *Zarathustra*, 162.
14. See Bash, *Ethics*, 169–73.

of behavior, such as pardon, amnesty, or condonation, does not exist outside philosophers' musings.

Another way of looking at this is to say that forgiveness tends to be either "thick forgiveness" (when it is more like "pure forgiveness") or "thin forgiveness" (when it is less like "pure forgiveness") or somewhere in between.[15] Whichever of these ways we look at it, we chase a will-o'-the-wisp if we seek forgiveness that is uncompromised either by relations with the victim or by other patterns of behavior that seek to bring about restored relationships. (I am hard-pressed to think of any pattern of behavior that can be said to exist in "pure" form.) We can go further: often, even divine forgiveness does not appear to be "pure," for in the Hebrew Scriptures, divine forgiveness is usually predicated on human repentance.

If we want a theology of forgiveness that is rooted in the biblical traditions and that accords with moral sensibilities, the question is not, "How can we offer 'pure' forgiveness?" as Derrida asks (for probably only God can do that, and we are not God) but, "What are the characteristics of forgiving behavior, and how do we recognize them?" This is one of the principal questions we explore in this book. In effect, what I am saying is that forgiveness is polyvalent, that is, it has a variety of forms and facets. Each situation must be looked at in its context to see if what we regard as forgiveness—even if thinly textured—is present.

BROKERS OF DIVINE FORGIVENESS

The Christian Scriptures bear evidence of early church practices about giving and receiving divine forgiveness. Books have been written about the practices, and I can no

15. Bash, *Just Forgiveness*, 35–40.

more than outline some of the main issues and solutions in this section.

Principally, we see evidence that individuals gave and withheld divine forgiveness on behalf of God. The earliest written evidence of this pattern of thinking is mid-first century in 1 Cor 4:3–5. In this passage (the meaning of which is difficult to understand), Paul writes about a man who had had sexual relations with his stepmother. He tells the Corinthians to hand over the man "to Satan for the destruction of the flesh" (v. 5) and says that when the Corinthians do this he would be "present in spirit." Paul also says that he had "already pronounced judgment" on the man.

Within the field of biblical studies, there is considerable discussion about what Paul means here; the commentaries set out a range of interpretations. Less talked about within biblical studies (but not in the fields of ecclesiology and church history) is Paul's claim in this passage to have the power to administer discipline and even punishment, perhaps on behalf of God. (Verse 4 is ambiguous as to whether Paul exercises institutional power, as a member of the church, or power, on behalf of God, by virtue of his calling as an apostle.)

The same ambiguity is in evidence in Matt 16:19 and 18:18, late first-century passages that, if taken at face value, have their roots in Jesus's teaching. As there are references to "church" (16:18 and 18:17), the text will almost certainly have been adapted to reflect early church thought and practice that developed after the death of Jesus. What was said at the time is now next to impossible to establish with certainty. The two Matthean passages indicate that church leaders, or perhaps Peter alone, have the power "to bind" and "to loose" on earth and in heaven. (One of the points of debate is to establish whether to "bind" and "loose" are instances of a wider authority bestowed by having the "keys of the kingdom of heaven.") This power has been interpreted as including the power to forgive and to withhold divine forgiveness. The link with the apostles' power to broker divine forgiveness is spelt out in John 20:23 (the only explicit reference to forgiveness in John's Gospel), which seems to be an adaptation of the Matthean passages about binding and loosing.

I cannot hide my unease about the supposed power of Peter, perhaps also of the apostles, and especially of so-called "apostolic successors" of Peter, to broker divine forgiveness. On my reading of the Christian Scriptures, divine forgiveness is a gift of grace from God. Apart from in contentious and obscure passages that bear the hallmarks of recension by the early church, I see no basis for the supposed power to bind and loose sins. I suspect the power was developed as an instrument of church discipline out of an obscure saying of Jesus that has been taken out of context. It is significant that Paul does not allude to the power to "bind" and "loose," and, if he had known about it, I suspect he would have gladly quoted it to lend support to his apostolic ministry. Paul's failure to mention the power reinforces my view that the power is a late addition to the Gospels' traditions.

QUESTIONS

1. Which reasons have been suggested for saying that God cannot forgive? How might we respond?

2. Which reasons have been suggested for saying that human beings cannot forgive? How might we respond?

3. Do you think that people can be brokers of divine forgiveness? Why or why not?

PART 2

TEXTUAL QUESTIONS

Chapter 9

PAUL AND FORGIVENESS

WE START OUR EXPLORATION of the Christian Scriptures on forgiveness with the "undisputed" writings of Paul, because they are the first documents in the Christian Scriptures to have been written, though no doubt oral accounts of Jesus's life and teaching were by then in circulation and known about.

THE SEVEN UNDISPUTED LETTERS

Imagine, for a moment, that all that we have in the Christian Scriptures were the seven undisputed letters of Paul. What sort of a theology of interpersonal forgiveness might we come up with?

I think, first, we would say that interpersonal forgiveness does not appear much in evidence in Paul's writings. In fact, there is remarkably little explicitly on interpersonal forgiveness in Paul.[1] Next, we would notice too that each time Paul writes of interpersonal forgiveness, he uses the same word, *charizomai*. The root of the word *charizomai* has to do with "grace" and "gift." When Paul uses *charizomai* other than to refer to "forgiveness," he is alluding

1. See 2 Cor 2:7, 10 and 12:13.

to the lavish generosity of God.[2] When Paul uses the word to refer to interpersonal forgiveness, he is thinking of a gift of kindness and mercy that one person gives another, probably as part of the way that people live out the grace of God they have received. (Note, in contrast, that elsewhere in the Christian Scriptures, and in the Gospels in particular, *aphiēmi* and *aphesis*, not *charizomai*, are almost always used for interpersonal forgiveness.) Third, Paul does not use the other words for interpersonal forgiveness, *synginōskō* and *syngnōmē*, which people used at the time. (Paul does use *syngnōmē* once, but not in the sense of "forgive" or "forgiveness.") Last, Paul refers to divine forgiveness by several different words only in Rom 4:7, and not with *charizomai*. (We discuss this verse and its significance in chapter 14.) In view of these four observations, we can say at this stage that forgiveness at first sight appears to be relatively unimportant to Paul, no more than a footnote in his thought, that compared to other places in the Christian Scriptures Paul's language about forgiveness is idiosyncratic, and that Paul seems to draw a distinction between interpersonal forgiveness (which he expresses with one word) and divine forgiveness (which, in the one verse he refers to it, he expresses with others).

EXPLICIT REFERENCES TO FORGIVENESS

In the first of the two passages where Paul refers to interpersonal forgiveness (2 Cor 2:7, 10) Paul urges the Corinthians to welcome back into the community a former member who had been expelled for a serious offence. Scholars speculate about what the offence may have been, and many think that the person who had been excluded is the man referred

2. See Rom 8:32, 1 Cor 2:12, Gal 3:18, Phil 1:29, 2:9, and (depending on one's viewpoint!) Phlm 22.

to in 1 Cor 5:1–5, who had had sexual relations with his stepmother. The offender was distressed by the punishment, and it seems he was in danger of being "overcome by excessive sorrow." Paul reassures the community that he would support a decision by the Corinthians to readmit the offender; he also says "if" he has forgiven the offender at all (by "if" Paul seems to imply there is doubt in his mind that forgiveness is the appropriate term for responding to what the offender has done), it is for the sake of the good of the community. Using the word that occurs in all modern translations, Paul urges the Corinthians to "forgive" the man because he has been punished enough.

In effect, what Paul urges the Corinthians to do is to welcome back the man, and to give him a generous welcome, because he is now contrite and remorseful. "Forgiveness" in this context means that the community offers the offender a new start within the community. The new start includes what today we would call "pastoral support," for Paul urges the community to give the man "comfort" (the word can also be translated "encouragement"), as he was in danger of being overwhelmed by shame. In effect, what Paul is urging the Corinthians to do is to show favor and kindness to the man. (Interestingly, "to show favor and kindness" is the principal classical Greek meaning of the word *charizomai*.) The Corinthians are to practice toward the man the grace and mercy which they themselves had received from God and they are to do this by "giving a gift of grace" (this is how *charizomai* can be translated) to the man. As for Paul's own supposed forgiveness, he more-or-less admits he has nothing to forgive, because, so we can assume, he has not himself been wronged and because the man had been disciplined. His offer to forgive, such as it is, is that he will put behind him the memory and lingering disappointment about what happened, and regard the matter as closed. Paul extends the idea of forgiveness to being something that a community, and not just individuals, can offer.

The other passage where Paul speaks of interpersonal forgiveness is 2 Cor 12:13. Paul is referring to the fact that he did not ask the Corinthians for financial support, whereas it appears those whom he calls "super-apostles," and whom the Corinthians so greatly admired, did ask for, and accept, financial support. The Corinthians seem to think that Paul was a second-rate apostle because he had neither sought nor received financial support from them. He writes to assure the Corinthians that he was in no way inferior to the "super-apostles." He notionally agrees that if he were the same as the super-apostles he should have accepted support, and so apologizes for the supposed wrong of not accepting support. However, the point of his argument is that he is not the same as the super-apostles; rather, the super-apostles, according to Paul, pervert the very idea of authentic apostleship. Paul's apology, such as it is, is given in the context of what is called an "*ad hominem* argument," that is, an argument that assumes the premises of one's opponents. Seen this way, the apology is in fact not an apology at all and the entreaty to forgive a rhetorical ploy.

IMPLICIT REFERENCES TO FORGIVENESS

Can we say, from Paul's letters, that the idea of interpersonal forgiveness is implicit in Paul's thought, perhaps not so much evidenced in specific words or phrases, but seen more in Paul's tone, demeanor, or example?

One understated example is Paul's request to Philemon to take back and welcome home Philemon's slave, Onesimus. It appears Onesimus had wronged Philemon. Paul offers to repay anything that is owing to Philemon as a result of Onesimus's wrongdoing. In effect, Paul is urging

Philemon to forgive Onesimus for his wrongdoing, and is offering to make reparation on Onesimus's behalf because, presumably, Onesimus lacked the means to do this. This is not a typical example of forgiveness: the restitution and the appeal for forgiveness are proxy (made by Paul, a third party, and not by Onesimus) and we do not know what Onesimus himself thought or wanted.

In other places, evidence of interpersonal forgiveness is lacking in situations where one might have expected to find it. Paul sometimes comes across not only as unforgiving, but also as combative and disputatious. (One gets the same impression of Paul from Luke's record of him in Acts.) For example, Paul insists in 1 Cor 5 that the Corinthians are to "hand over to Satan for the destruction of the flesh" the man who had sexual relations with his stepmother. He also writes of "punishing" disobedience (2 Cor 10:6), of not being "lenient" (2 Cor 13:2), and of being "severe" in the use of the authority God has given him (2 Cor 13:10). The Corinthians are also to shun anyone who is "sexually immoral, greedy, an idolater, a slanderer, a drunkard, or swindler" (1 Cor 5:11). Paul affirms that divisions and disagreements can be necessary (1 Cor 11:19), but says nothing about how to resolve them. He writes letters that distress his readers and seems equivocal about whether he is sorry (2 Cor 7:8). These are not examples of constructive community building or evidence of a forgiving spirit.

Although Paul may not always be the most compelling example of someone who modeled a loving and forgiving spirit (and admittedly the situations he faced in some of his letters would have taxed the most longsuffering of people), on many occasions Paul did model it. For example, many parts of his letters to Philemon and to the Philippians, and of his first letter to the Thessalonians, show the love that he had for the churches he had founded and the people who comprised them. Paul can be warm, a kind encourager, and a patient pastor. When crossed, under threat, or believing that the gospel is being compromised, he could be as confrontational and cantankerous as one dare imagine of a Christian leader.

PAUL, FORGIVENESS, AND LOVE

Forgiveness is clearly not a major category of Paul's thought, and we do an injustice to his thought if we seek to read Paul as a theologian of forgiveness. This is surprising, given that, as we shall see in chapters 10–12, forgiveness appears to be important in the thought and teaching of Jesus. Paul's preferred categories of thought are justification and grace, (which is reflected in his use of the word *charizomai* and that we sometimes translate as "forgive").

The infrequency of references to forgiveness in Paul's writings takes us to the much-disputed question of how much Paul knew of Jesus's teachings. Does the fact that Paul does not say much about forgiveness indicate that he did not know the Gospels' traditions about forgiveness?

I am confident Paul knew something of the oral traditions about Jesus that would have been circulating when he wrote his letters; on one occasion he even quotes from them. The reason for Paul's reluctance to write about forgiveness is, I suggest, not so much that Paul did not know about the earlier Christian traditions on forgiveness as that forgiveness, in the way the early Christians thought about it, does not fit easily with the way Paul had come to understand salvation and ethics. We explore this important observation further in chapter 14.

What Paul shares with the teaching of Jesus is an emphasis on love. In Paul's theology, as in Jesus's, love is the underlying, guiding principle of all behavior. For Paul, love is the fulfilling of "the law" and the rationale of the way people should behave toward one another (Rom 13:8, 10; Gal 5:14). All Paul's ethical injunctions can be subsumed under the rubric of love. This includes not being vengeful (Rom 12:19), not repaying evil for evil (1 Thess 5:15), and being at peace with one another (1 Thess 5:13). These are aspects of what, in other places, are said to be characteristics of forgiving behavior.

Paul is strongly community-minded in his theology (not surprisingly, as he was writing to communities) and he writes about love in the context of its outworking in communities. When we discern he could be referring to forgiveness in his writings, we usually find that he is in fact writing about love.

We return to the question we began with at the start of this chapter: if all we had were the seven undisputed letters of Paul, what sort of a theology of forgiveness might we now have? The answer is probably that we would not be speaking and writing of "forgiving behavior." In fact, we would not have a theology of forgiveness at all, but (and this is surely as good, and perhaps better) a theology of love.

THE SIX DISPUTED LETTERS

When we turn to the "disputed" letters, there are points of similarity and also some developments. Only Ephesians and Colossians refer to forgiveness.[3] In Eph 1:7 and Col 1:14, the writer, whom I shall refer to as "Paul," links divine forgiveness (*aphesis*) and the atonement. In these verses, the emphasis has moved from justification, which we see in the undisputed letters, to forgiveness as an outcome of the atonement. *Charizomai* is used of divine forgiveness in Col

---

3. Eph 1:7, Col 1:14 (*aphesis*), Eph 4:32, Col 2:13, 3:13 (*charizomai*).

2:13, and in the next verse Paul explains divine forgiveness as being like erasing the legal record of debts that are owed. Here forgiveness is like a gift (in 2:13) and like remission of debt (in 2:14).

As for Christian behavior, the pattern of logic in Ephesians and Colossians is that by their behavior, Christians are to practice the virtues of God. Thus, since God is loving, Christians are to be loving (Eph 5:2); since God is forgiving, Christians are to be forgiving (Eph 4:32, Col 3:13). In other words, Christians are to live imitatively of the grace of forgiveness they have received. Note that the word for forgiveness in the two entreaties to forgive (Eph 4:32 and Col 3:13) is *charizomai*, pointing to the lavish grace of God in Christ as the reason and motivation to be forgiving. One could equally well translate *charizomai* in these verses as "be gracious."

Familiarity with this type of exhortation in the Christian Scriptures has dulled many to its logical impossibility, for it is not possible to derive an imperative ("be forgiving") from an indicative ("God forgives"). The difficulty can be easily illustrated from this example: it is (perhaps good advice but) illogical to say "I like chocolate; therefore you should like chocolate." Logically, the last sentence is no different from saying, for example, "God forgives; therefore you should forgive."

SUMMARY

We have seen how Paul's thought develops. In Paul's early writings, interpersonal forgiveness is not much in evidence as a discrete category of Christian ethical behavior; of more interest to Paul is the command to love, and that Christians should model in their relations with others the grace of Christ that they have received. The words we translate as "forgive" or "forgiveness" are really about God's grace lived out in the lives of human beings. In later developments of Paul's thought, forgiveness remains an expression of grace. The rationale of interpersonal forgiveness is that Christians are to be forgiving because God is forgiving. Even so, it can still sometimes be difficult to decide whether uppermost in Paul's mind is love, or grace, or forgiveness.

QUESTIONS

1. What does Paul mean by forgiveness?
2. In Paul's thought, what is the relationship of forgiveness and love to each other?
3. How does Paul's thought about forgiveness develop in the thirteen letters attributed to him?

Chapter 10

FORGIVENESS
IN THE GOSPEL OF MARK

AFTER PAUL'S WRITINGS, THE Gospel of Mark is regarded as next to have been written. It is difficult to be certain when the Gospel was written: Joel Marcus suggests it was between 69–75 CE, and this is almost certainly right from the internal evidence of the Gospel.[1]

It is very likely that Mark drew on "oral traditions" that were in existence even before Paul wrote his letters. However, these traditions will have been developed by the early church, and also redacted (edited) by Mark when he wrote the Gospel. This means that the Gospel is likely to have a substratum of very early material, and also later accretions to that material. Despite academics' best endeavors, there is little agreement about how to identify the relative ages of the material in the Gospel or the extent to which earlier traditions have been modified and adapted.

Every reference to forgiveness in the Gospel of Mark, whether the reference is to interpersonal forgiveness or to God's forgiveness, is either with the verb *aphiēmi* (2:5, 7, 9, 10; 3:28; 4:12; 11:25, [26]) or with the noun *aphesis* (1:4,

1. Marcus, *Mark 1–8*, 39.

3:9). This suggests that Mark was following the traditional pattern of language about forgiveness in the Septuagint and not drawing on the language of secular, Hellenistic Greek. He was also perhaps not aware of Paul's use of *charizomai*.

INTERPERSONAL FORGIVENESS

There is only one verse (possibly two, if one accepts a disputed reading) on interpersonal forgiveness in the Gospel (Mark 11:25, and perhaps 11:26).

The first part of Mark 11:25 unequivocally asserts that people are to forgive "anyone" against whom they have "anything." This most likely reflects and reinforces a development in Judaism in the second and first centuries BCE, which we see, for example, reflected in Sir 28:2a.[2] Additionally, and equally importantly, the second half of the verse insists that such people must be forgivers if they are also to receive God's forgiveness. (The doubtful reading in v. 26, which no more than states the converse of v. 25, is unlikely to be part of the original text, but, according to Bruce Metzger, a scribal insertion "in imitation of Matt 6:15."[3]) Thus Jesus makes divine forgiveness and interpersonal forgiveness co-dependent. This reflects Sir 28:2b, which assures those who have forgiven their neighbor that their "sins will be pardoned when [they] pray." Note the contrast with Paul in these verses: with Paul, those who have received grace are themselves to be vehicles of grace to others (2 Cor 1:3–7), and, by implication, those who have been forgiven are themselves, as recipients of grace, to practice the grace of forgiveness toward others. In contrast, Jesus in

2. A translation of Sir 28:2a is: "Forgive the wrongdoing your neighbor has done to you."

3. Metzger, *Textual Commentary*, 110.

Mark's Gospel says that those who are unforgiving will not receive God's forgiveness.

On the face of it, it appears that Jesus insists people are to forgive unrepentant wrongdoers. If they do not, they will be regarded an unforgiving, and so at risk of cutting themselves off from God's forgiveness. I have already explained in chapter 5 why this is not likely to be the case. There are also two additional reasons. Some who have been wronged will be so deeply traumatized that they are not able to forgive. It is not the case that they do not want to forgive; it is that they cannot. It is psychologically naïve to say that such people could and should forgive, if only they would try harder. I doubt that God denies divine forgiveness to people who are damaged in this way and cannot forgive. Secondly, we also need to remember that Jesus often spoke hyperbolically in order to make what he said easily memorable. Jesus sought to leave his hearers with a straightforward way to remember that being forgiven and forgiving others are conjoined. In making a hyperbolic statement, Jesus was not negating what else is true of forgiving and of being forgiven.

Does Mark's approach to forgiveness make sense from a theological, pastoral, and psychological point of view? I think it does, because to be "knotted" with anger, bitterness, and resentment is a sure block to receiving any expression of grace, including forgiveness. If we are not forgivers, or seeking to be forgivers, we will not be in a frame of mind to seek forgiveness ourselves.

We are still left with a disquieting observation. Interpersonal forgiveness in the Gospel of Mark appears to be not much more than a passing topic and hardly a characteristic axiom of Christian behavior. If we ask of the Gospel the same question that we asked of Paul, namely, "If all that we had were the Gospel of Mark, what sort of a theology of interpersonal forgiveness might we come up with?" we would apparently not have much to say. However, despite the paucity of explicit references to forgiveness, Mark's interest in interpersonal forgiveness, if set in the broader context of the Gospel, is much more extensive and thoughtful than the few words of Mark 11:25–26 suggest. We now turn to the broader context and see that it is easy, without that broader context, to understate the significance of interpersonal forgiveness in Mark's Gospel.

DIVINE FORGIVENESS

The opening words of Mark's Gospel tell the reader that the Gospel is about "the good news of Jesus Christ." This good news is both the subject matter of what Jesus preached, as well as Jesus himself being the good news. The good news is that a decisive point in history, the coming of the kingdom of God, had come about in, by, and through the person and ministry of Jesus (1:14–15) who gave himself as a "ransom" (10:45) to establish that kingdom. The rest of the Gospel points to what will characterize the kingdom, and gives signs and evidence of its imminent coming. We learn that when the kingdom has been established, God will have triumphed over the hidden, demonic forces that control the world and some of its people, and established a new order for human living. Illness and suffering, often understood to be the result of demonic influence, will have ended. Of particular interest to us is that in the new order of the kingdom, sins are forgiven (4:12). There is a foretaste of those future realities in the ministry of Jesus in the Gospel: in other words, the future certainties of the kingdom are, to some extent, brought into and experienced in the present. So when in Mark 2:5 Jesus says that the sins of the paralytic are "forgiven," he is pointing to a future reality of which the paralytic could be certain and which he could, to some extent, also experience in the present.

In preparation for the coming kingdom, John the Baptist told the people to repent "for the forgiveness of sins" (1:4). I take the latter phrase to mean that the people's sins would be forgiven when the kingdom comes. (You will realize from this that I understand John to mean not that his baptism brought about forgiveness but that his baptism was "with a view to" the forthcoming forgiveness. In other words, forgiveness is an expectation for those who participate in the future kingdom.) Jesus says much the same in 1:15: the people were to repent because the time of waiting for the kingdom was over. The rest of the sentence goes unsaid, but it is obvious what it is, namely, that when the kingdom comes, the people's sins would be forgiven if they were ready. The link between the kingdom, forgiveness, and repentance is also explicitly made in 4:12, although this aspect of 4:12 tends to be overlooked in commentaries because it is set in the context of some unrelated, complicated, theological questions about the messianic secret, God's election, and the reason for parables.

In view of what Mark says about the kingdom, it is not surprising that illness and sin, and their flip-side, healing and forgiveness, are often thought about together. It was therefore neither easier nor harder for Jesus to heal the paralyzed man at Capernaum than to forgive his sins (Mark 2:1–11). They are both proleptic experiences of the future kingdom, though only one of them, the healing, can be verified in the present. Jesus healed the man and declared the man's forgiveness because Jesus, and not some other person, was the divine agent by whom the kingdom would be established. As Jesus says, he "had authority" to forgive (2:10), and by implication authority to heal, because he was

God's appointee through whom the decisive change in human affairs was being initiated and would be established.

The coming kingdom points to the abolition of the temple and its practices, for the forgiveness of the kingdom was not brokered through temple priests, but was for all who responded to the call of Jesus. Although Mark's Gospel does not say this explicitly, it is implicit that the forgiveness of the kingdom is qualitatively different from the forgiveness brought about through the temple offerings, because even those who did make offerings in the temple still needed the forgiveness of the kingdom. As we shall see in chapter 13, the writer to the Hebrews takes up and explores this further, using the idea of new covenant, not kingdom.

God's future forgiveness is of all sins and any blasphemies people utter (3:28). There is nothing outside the scope of God's forgiveness, except "blasphemy against the Holy Spirit," which is "an eternal sin" (3:29). This fits with Jewish theology generally, which held that every sin could be atoned for except the rejection of God and the Jewish covenant with God.[4] In the context of Mark's Gospel, blasphemy against the Holy Spirit is to reject God and, in the context of 3:28–29 (and of its parallel in Matthew's Gospel, but not Luke's Gospel), it means to ascribe the source of Jesus's power not to the Holy Spirit but to demonic forces (3:22, 30). As in 2:7, a person who has such a complete misunderstanding of Jesus, of the source of his power, and of God (whose agent Jesus is) in effect rejects God and God's covenant, and so is guilty of inexpiable sin.

Forgiveness is one of the characteristic markers of the kingdom of God. It is therefore not surprising that those who are members of that kingdom, whose lives and being are re-shaped and transformed by it, are themselves to be forgivers. What sort of a kingdom would it be if its

4. Sanders, *Paul*, 157.

members were all forgiven but personally characterized by bile, bitterness, and anger, hating other people, and being hateful toward them? Of course, the kingdom's members must forgive if they have "anything against anyone" because otherwise they would compromise, and even pervert, the very idea of being members of the kingdom of God.

If we return to our question, "If all that we had were the Gospel of Mark, what sort of a theology of interpersonal forgiveness might we come up with?" the answer would be as follows: God's forgiveness is constitutive of the kingdom, and the members of the kingdom are to live congruently with the ethics of the kingdom. This means that, like God, they are to be forgivers. If they are not forgivers, they repudiate the very basis of being members of the kingdom.

QUESTIONS

1. What is Mark's theology of forgiveness?
2. What is the significance of interpersonal forgiveness in the Gospel of Mark?

Chapter 11

FORGIVENESS IN LUKE-ACTS

IN HIS COMMENTARY ON Luke's Gospel, Christopher Evans sets the writing of the Gospel between 75–130 CE.[1] The Gospel is therefore almost certainly written after Mark's Gospel, though we cannot be sure whether it was written before or after Matthew's Gospel.

Most likely, the same person is the author of both the Gospel of Luke and the Acts of the Apostles. The author is usually referred to as "Luke" and the two books as "Luke-Acts." When I refer to the Gospel alone, I call it "Luke" or "the Gospel of Luke."

A quick read of the Gospel of Luke discloses that Luke incorporated into his Gospel much of the Gospel of Mark, as well as having some material either of his own (tradition-ally referred to as coming from a source or sources called "L") or which he shares with Matthew (which scholars call "Q"). Luke himself says in the introduction to the Gospel that his account is based on careful use of the reports of eyewitnesses and of early Christian ministers (Luke 1:2). So it is plausible that Luke knew Mark's Gospel, had access

1. Evans, *Luke*, 14.

to other material, whether oral or written, and was writing what we today would regard as a carefully researched account, based on sources that were contemporaneous with the events he describes.

Interpreting the Gospel with these suppositions about the source-material Luke used can help us to identify Luke's editorial intentions, and so his particular interests and emphases. It can point us to how and when Luke modified material that is found in Mark; it can also point us to what Luke excludes from Mark. Asking why Luke made these editorial changes may suggest what is distinctive about Luke's theology of forgiveness. For similar reasons, we will be able to identify what Luke leaves unchanged: the fact that some material is apparently deliberately unchanged, or edited in only minor ways, suggests it has an important place in Luke's theology of forgiveness, just as it may have in other Gospels where it is found.

Despite Luke's probable use of Mark's Gospel and the presence of material they share, Luke subtly changes the emphasis he inherits from Mark's Gospel. The result is that Luke's Gospel is a work with a different feel, and with different theological emphases. As with Mark, there is not a great deal explicitly about interpersonal forgiveness.[2] Nevertheless, we have reason to say, as we shall see later, that, of the writers of the Christian Scriptures, Luke is one of two theologians of forgiveness *par excellence*. The other, as we shall see, is Matthew.

INTERPERSONAL FORGIVENESS

Of Luke's four explicit references to interpersonal forgiveness (which are all in the Gospel), Luke 23:34 ("Father,

2. Luke 6:37; 11:4; 17:3–4; and, if part of the text, 23:34. Mark 11:25–26 is not in Luke's Gospel.

forgive them, for they do not know what they are doing") is
a disputed reading. The verse is in some of the best manuscripts, and not in other of the best manuscripts. It is probably one of the best known of all verses in the Christian
Scriptures. Bruce Metzger's conclusion is that the verse
"though probably not a part of the original Greek of Luke,
bears self-evident tokens of its dominical origin" and so has
been "incorporated by unknown copyists relatively early in
the transmission" of the Gospel.[3]

The verse is commonly (but mistakenly) referred to as
Jesus's prayer of "forgiveness" on the cross. It is reflected in
Stephen's prayer in Acts 7:60 as he was dying. We have already discussed Luke 23:34 and Acts 7:60 in chapter 5, and
pointed out that, by their prayers, both Jesus and Stephen
exemplify a spirit that eschews revenge, and seeks the best
for their enemies. In this way the prayers model Jesus's own
teaching that we find, for example, in Luke 6:27–37. Nevertheless, the prayers are not prayers that God would forgive
unrepentant wrongdoers. In addition, neither passage sup-
ports the suggestion that one should forgive unrepentant
wrongdoers, or leaves open the possibility that, in offering
forgiveness, Christians thereby hang up their integrity or
connive with or condone wrongdoing.

Of the other three references to interpersonal forgiveness in the Gospel, Luke 17:3–4 has echoes of Matt 18:15,
21–22 but is clearly from a different source. Jesus states in
verse 3 that if one's brother repents (meaning by "brother,"
of course, not a male sibling only, but a fellow believer of
either sex), one should forgive that person. The emphasis
is different from Mark 11:25–26, which we explored in the
last chapter: in Mark, the emphasis is on the victim taking initiative to forgive, whereas in Luke the emphasis is on
the wrongdoer repenting and taking the initiative to seek

---

3. Metzger, *Textual Commentary*, 180.

forgiveness. In verse 4, Jesus says that "if the same person sins against you seven times a day," one must forgive that person, if he or she is repentant, every time that person seeks forgiveness. (If one stops to think carefully, to be wronged seven times in one day could amount to a dreadful measure of trauma. This suggests that the verse is another example of Jesus teaching in hyperbole to make what he said memorable.)

Two implications arise from what Jesus says in 17:4. First, forgiveness should not be limited, reluctant, or conditional with a forgiver apparently saying or implying before offering forgiveness, "I will forgive you on this one occasion, but if you wrong me again I will not forgive you." Second, people are to forgive repentant wrongdoers, no matter how difficult it may seem and no matter what the personal cost, because the practice of interpersonal forgiveness is one of the paramount characteristics of being a follower of Jesus.

The other two verses on interpersonal forgiveness link forgiving others with being forgiven oneself. They do not state that repentance is a precondition of forgiveness, though one should not think otherwise, because in the rest of Luke-Acts repentance and forgiveness are almost always linked.[4] The first of the two verses is Luke 6:37. Jesus states baldly, "Forgive ['set free'], and you will be forgiven ['be set free']." (This is the only place in the Gospel where Luke does not use *aphiēmi* or *aphesis* for "forgive" and "forgiveness." Instead, Luke uses the verb *apoluō*.) The second is Luke 11:4, which is from Luke's version of the Lord's Prayer and which has parallels in Mark 11:23. It grounds a prayer for divine forgiveness on the fact that the supplicant is a forgiver. The words of Luke 11:4 are ". . . forgive us our sins, for we ourselves forgive all indebted to us." (I explained in chapter 3 that debt is a metaphor for sin.) At these points,

4. See, e.g., Luke 3:3; 17:3–4; 24:37; Acts 2:38; 5:31; 8:22; and 26:18.

Luke is theologically similar to Mark and the point is clear: forgiving others and being forgiven go together.

Looking at these four passages on interpersonal forgiveness together, we can summarize Luke's theology of interpersonal forgiveness in this way: forgiveness is about not taking revenge but seeking the best for one's enemies. It is always unconditionally to forgive the repentant, without regard to how difficult or personally costly it may be. People who forgive can look to God to forgive them; by implication, those who do not forgive others will not themselves receive God's forgiveness.

In these respects, Luke and Mark are self-consistent; we might say that Luke more strongly emphasizes repentance than Mark, but apart from that, we come away with conclusions that are much the same. What is different—significantly different—is the theological context in which Luke sets interpersonal forgiveness. To this we now turn.

THEOLOGICAL CONTEXT

The organizing key to Mark's theology of forgiveness is the kingdom of God and what that means. Not so, with Luke. For Luke, what is central is that Jesus is "the Christ" (Messiah) (Luke 2:11).[5] In Luke's Gospel, the Messiah is the savior (Luke 2:11) who brings *aphesis*, that is, forgiveness of or release from sins (Luke 1:77). Thus, Simeon was promised he would see the "Messiah" before his death (Luke 2:26); the Messiah was the "salvation" (Luke 2:30) for all the peoples of the world. Similarly, John the Baptist's ministry was to prepare the way for the one who would bring the promised "salvation" (Luke 3:6). John insisted that he was "not the Messiah"; rather the Messiah was the one for whose way he was preparing (Luke 3:15–17). The Messiah in Luke's

5. See also Luke 3:15; 4:41; 9:20; 20:41–44; 22:67; 23:2, 35; 24:26, 46.

writings reconstitutes the people of God, so that its identity comes not from Jerusalem and the temple, an identity that we see so clearly at the start of the Gospel, but from the response of individuals to Jesus and, in the period after the Holy Spirit had been given, by baptism into the Spirit. It is by believing in Jesus that people are saved and forgiven (Acts 10:43, 13:38, for example).

The savior brings *aphesis*, not only of sins but also of much more. In Luke, *aphesis* principally means "release," that is, release from sin, from illness and death, from demonic forces, from oppression, and from injustice. Two examples that are not of release from sin illustrate this. In Luke 4:16–30, the first example, Jesus quotes from a pastiche of verses loosely based on Isa 61 and 58 about an anointed person who brings *aphesis* (release) for prisoners. The same verse speaks of "freedom" for the oppressed. Significantly, Jesus says that the verses from Isaiah that he quotes "have been fulfilled" in the hearing of his listeners. By this he means that he is the anointed person whose coming brings release and completes Jewish messianic expectations. The second example is of the woman whom Jesus healed of spinal scoliosis. He said she had been "bound" by Satan. In healing her, Jesus said he had made her "free from the imprisonment" of the disease (Luke 13:16). The good news of Luke's Gospel is that Jesus, the Messiah and savior, brings freedom for and release to a world in the thrall of Satan.

DIVINE FORGIVENESS

Words for "forgiveness" do not occur in the parable of the Prodigal Son (Luke 15:11–32). Nevertheless, many regard the parable as having much to say about forgiveness because in the parable the father welcomes back his errant son.

Almost certainly and from its context in the Gospel, the parable is about the fact that God restores to the community of faith Jewish people, such as "tax-collectors and sinners" (15:1) (typologically represented by the younger son), who have excluded themselves from the community by sin. The father unconditionally welcomes back the younger son when he (the younger son) returns in penitence and remorse. The point is that there is nothing people can do, even repudiating their former place in the covenant, which can take them outside God's welcoming mercy and love. The only condition for return is that they want to return, seek to return, and return in penitence.

I suspect some did not welcome the parable because they thought Jesus was teaching that God favored the faithless and disobedient. The older son in the parable represents such critics. He was angry with his father for throwing a party for a younger brother who, in the older son's opinion, deserved punishment and condemnation. Jesus highlights the older son's self-pitying, judgmental attitude, and thereby exposes the self-pity and judgmentalism of Jesus's own hearers toward "tax-collectors and sinners." In response, and by means of the parable, Jesus assures those who criticized him for extending mercy and welcome to "tax-collectors and sinners" that their (the critics') place in the covenant is secure and that God's love for them remains undimmed. What Jesus means is that though there is rejoicing over lost sinners who return, it is not at the expense of continued rejoicing over those who never left.

There are two lessons about forgiveness for Jesus's hearers here. Obviously, there is the father's welcome of the younger son's return. The point is that as God welcomes all people who wish to return, so human beings should welcome and forgive those who wish to put right past wrongs. It is the principle of Luke 17:3, this time in parabolic form:

". . . if there is repentance, you must forgive." The second lesson, which is not usually brought out with clarity, is that the older son must learn to forgive too. Forgiveness is a gift for the undeserving and for failures. It should not be withheld as a way of showing one's disapproval of what a wrongdoer has done. The older son, therefore, needed to welcome home, and forgive, his younger brother.

The place of "tax-collectors and sinners" and their relationship to the "righteous" is also explored in Luke 7:36–50, the story of the woman with ointment who outlandishly and extravagantly anointed Jesus's feet at the house of Simon, a Pharisee.

Simon is deeply critical that Jesus allowed himself to be anointed by a "sinner"—and a woman sinner at that. Jesus tells a parable that simply demonstrates, by analogy with money debt, that the more one is forgiven, the more one responds with gratitude. Jesus then explains that the woman's actions are lavish because she believed she had done much that was wrong and had received much forgiveness; she knew that the measure of her forgiveness corresponded with the measure of her wrongdoing.[6] Although Luke does not make this link (but Matthew does as we shall see in the next chapter when we consider Matt 18:23–35), one can imagine that the woman will herself also be a forgiving person, because of her own experience of being forgiven.

There is a "sting in the tail" for Simon, the Pharisee to whom Jesus is speaking. Jesus points out to Simon that,

6. I am confident this is the correct interpretation of the parable, and modern Bible translations and commentaries support this interpretation. The word *hoti* in v. 47, if translated "because" (as one would expect), presents enormous difficulties for this interpretation, as it suggests that the woman was forgiven much *because* she loved much. I explore the difficulties in Bash, *Ethics*, 96–97, and *Just Forgiveness*, 92–96.

compared with the woman, he (Simon) had been relatively unwelcoming and inhospitable. More than that, because he was not a "sinner" like the woman, he had failed to realize that he was critical about her, and perhaps even smug and self-righteous. In other words, for all his righteousness, Simon too stood in need of forgiveness. One hopes that Simon came to see that, like the woman, he needed to be forgiven much, even though at the start of the story, if he had applied his mind to the question, he would have thought that he did not.

In some respects, Simon is like the older son in the parable of the Prodigal Son. Unlike the older son, he was not angry and self-pitying about another's forgiveness and inclusion; however, like the older son, he was critical of the grace extended to an unrighteous sinner. Both Simon and the older son were blind to their own need for forgiveness. A critical, bitter spirit (in the case of the older son) or self-righteous, critical disdain (in the case of Simon the Pharisee) can close off people from being forgiving, and can also close off those same people from seeing their own need for forgiveness and from the grace that forgiveness brings. Perhaps this observation helps us to make better sense of Luke 6:37 ("Forgive, and you will be forgiven") and Luke 11:4 (". . . forgive us our sins, for we ourselves forgive everyone indebted to us"): people who do not forgive others are often blind to their own need for forgiveness and so do not experience the grace that being forgiven can bring. To mix biblical imagery, they are so occupied about not forgiving others for the speck they see in those others' eyes that they fail to see their need to be forgiven for the log in their own eyes.

CONCLUDING OBSERVATIONS

If we were to ask Luke why people should forgive one another, Luke would answer, as would Mark, that divine forgiveness is contingent upon interpersonal forgiveness. "Always go on forgiving the repentant!" and "Forgivers will be forgiven!" could be their slogans.

For Luke, to forgive is a virtue and a duty at the core of Christian discipleship. In his view, human beings are to be merciful to the repentant, even if the repentant are otherwise also apparently undeserving, and to practice forgiving as God forgives. Luke highlights, in a way that Mark does not, that no one should be excluded from being forgiven if they are repentant.

Luke would add that one of the characteristics of the kingdom of God is God's *aphesis*—release, restoration, freedom, forgiveness, and so on—from all that shackles and constrains human beings. In other words, God's *aphesis* undoes what oppresses human beings and (we might add) puts right injustice, abuse, mistreatment, suffering, and brutality. God will also include outsiders who, in the present era of history, are excluded, and restore the "have nots" to their rightful place. Interpersonal forgiveness, Luke would say, mirrors God's forgiveness and offers a foretaste of the greater restorative work that God one day will complete. But note that with Luke it is not interpersonal forgiveness at any price: there must always be antecedent repentance to ensure, in some measure, that forgivers are themselves not oppressed by an overriding duty to forgive at the cost of a measure of justice for the forgivers themselves.

In addition, Luke's theology of interpersonal forgiveness is robust and psychologically astute. Luke perceptively points out that those who think they have little for which they need to be forgiven are mistaken; their sins may not be so egregious as some, but they have sins—usually of thought and motive rather than of deed—that are every bit in need of God's mercy as those whose outward actions deny them a place in the Jewish covenant.

QUESTIONS

1. What is Luke's theology of forgiveness?

2. What is the significance of interpersonal forgiveness in Luke-Acts?

3. How is Luke's theology of forgiveness different from Mark's?

Chapter 12

FORGIVENESS IN THE GOSPEL OF MATTHEW

LIKE LUKE, MATTHEW IS a creative theologian of forgiveness. He makes an important and distinctive contribution to a theology of forgiveness in the Christian Scriptures.

Before we look in detail at Matthew's theology of forgiveness, and in order to explain the rationale of the approach to the Gospel that I take, I will make a few introductory comments about the source-material scholars commonly believe Matthew used.

Although we do not know with certainty what exactly Matthew's source-material might be, careful analysis suggests that Matthew knew and included most of Mark's Gospel in his own Gospel. He also shares material with Luke, which Mark apparently did not know: as we saw in the last chapter, scholars call this material "Q." Matthew has his own source (or sources) of material, called "M." (Thus we assume at least two hypothetical sources, Q and M.) Most likely, Matthew was written after Luke, but whether or not this is so will not affect the conclusions of this chapter.

With this approach in mind, an initial read of Matthew in comparison with Mark and Luke discloses that Matthew sets Jesus in a distinctively Jewish setting, and places a strong emphasis on the Hebrew Scriptures. It is therefore not surprising that *aphiēmi* and *aphesis* are the only words Matthew uses for forgiveness: they are the words for forgiveness in the Septuagint, the Greek translation of the Hebrew Scriptures, with which Matthew is obviously familiar. We also notice that in the Gospel repentance is integral to forgiveness, just as it is in Mark and Luke, and in the Jewish tradition. Last, we become aware of one significant omission and two significant additions. The omission and the additions take us to what characterizes Matthew's theology of forgiveness. We now consider the omission and the two additions.

MATT 26:28

Perhaps most noteworthy of the additions is a short phrase ("for the forgiveness of sins") in Matt 26:28, which is part of the words of the institution of the Lord's Supper.

Jesus says the wine in the cup he holds represents his blood and says it is "the blood of the covenant." This phrase is an echo of the Hebrew Scriptures, where the idea of the phrase, referring to the blood of sacrifices, means a sign of the continuing covenant between God and the people of God that was evidenced by the people's loyalty to the temple sacrifices. Jesus adds that his blood is "poured out" (an allusion that we know to be to his imminent crucifixion) "for the forgiveness of sins." By these three phrases, Jesus links his death by crucifixion with a covenant and with forgiveness of sins. The other Gospels do not make the three-fold link, as they do not refer to forgiveness at this point.

The additional words "for the forgiveness of sins" point to Matthew's understanding of the death of Jesus: Jesus's death and God's forgiveness of sins are linked. Neither Mark nor Luke makes such an important connection so explicitly. Despite what is commonly thought, this is a development of the idea of sacrifices in the Hebrew Scriptures: the sacrifices were offered on behalf of the people to continue to renew the relationship between God and the people of God; they were also a way that the people expressed their continuing loyalty to God and the covenant. They were not offered for the forgiveness of sins and they were not thought of as substitutionary.

The allusion to a covenant is also important. Jesus uses words that would have suggested to his hearers the covenant at Sinai (Exod 24:5–8) that was sealed with animal blood. The Sinai covenant formed and shaped those who lived under it as the people of God. Jesus is suggesting that his death is like the death that established the earlier covenant at Sinai, a death that establishes a covenant that both forms and shapes those who live under the covenant. In other words, Jesus's death not only brings forgiveness but also melds forgiven people into the people of God.

MATT 3:1–2

Matthew omits from John the Baptist's preaching any indication that John's baptism is "for the forgiveness of sins" (Matt 3:1–2). Almost certainly, the reason is to ensure that the readers and hearers of the Gospel are left in no doubt that the covenant that is established through the death of Jesus—and only that covenant—bring salvation and forgiveness. Matthew wants to leave no room for question or error.

MATT 18:23–35

Besides the words in 26:28, there is another important addition to the Gospel. It is not a phrase, but a parable, the parable of the Unforgiving Servant (18:23–35), which is unique to this Gospel.

Jesus tells the parable in response to a question from Peter (18:21), who asks whether one should forgive wrong-doers even as many as seven times. We will consider Peter's question and Jesus's answer further, below. I mention it now, to put the parable in context.

The parable concerns two slaves. One slave owed a king ten thousand talents. The slave could not repay the debt and so the king decided to sell the slave, his family, and his possessions to repay the debt. The slave implored the king to spare him, and in response the king remitted the debt and let the slave go free.

The sum owed, as well as the story as a whole, is meant to be palpably absurd in terms of its factual plausibility. As for the ten thousand talents that were owed, Josephus says, for example, that the total tax Judaea remitted to Rome in a year was six thousand talents.[1] In addition, no king could (or would) have lent a slave as much as ten thousand talents, and no one could have repaid that much. To sell the slave and his family, as the king proposed to do, could not have raised enough to repay the debt. As we shall also shortly see, the story becomes even more implausible: the king later decides to revive the formerly canceled debt, and then sets out to realize the debt in full by torturing the slave. To say the least, the parable abounds in hyperbole, and this in part is what makes it so memorable.

So why does Jesus tell the parable? We have already explored the connection between money debts and sins, and between remission of debt and forgiveness of sins in chapter 3. With this in mind, we can say that up to this point in the parable, Jesus tells the parable to illustrate the

---

1. Josephus, *Ant.* 17.320.

lavish forgiveness of God, which he intends his hearers to understand is unimaginably generous.

The parable continues with an addition. The addition is about another slave who owes money to the first slave, the slave whose debts had been remitted. The amount owed is, relatively speaking, a mere one hundred denarii. We know from Matt 20:1–16 that a denarius is the daily wage of a laborer. In other words, the sum involved is equivalent to about three months' wages of a day laborer. This sum is trifling compared with the sum that the first slave had owed: the sum was equivalent to sixty million denarii. (I have calculated the sum on the basis that one talent corresponded to about six thousand denarii.) The first slave demands repayment of the loan. The second slave cannot repay the loan, and so the first slave throws the second slave into a debtors' prison, to remain there until the debt is paid in full. The king gets to hear of the first slave's lack of mercy. In fury at the first slave's lack of mercy, he hands over the first slave to be tortured until the first slave has repaid in full the former debt, now revived and once again due.

On the basis of what we know from the Gospels of Mark and Luke, we would expect the point of the parable to be something along these lines: the first slave should have been merciful and remitted the debt of the second slave. Otherwise, the first slave cannot expect mercy in the future, as there is a link between being merciful to others in the present and oneself receiving mercy in the future.

However, this is not the point of the parable. Rather, the king condemns the first slave because, though the first slave had himself received mercy, he failed to show mercy to his fellow slave. The parable insists that those who have received mercy are then to practice that mercy toward others. It understands mercy to be transformative grace for its recipients, and, if received in the way the giver intends it to be received, should become the basis of the recipients being merciful toward others. This is in keeping with the pattern of forgiveness in Paul's writings, but the reverse of the order in Mark and Luke, which is that those who show mercy will themselves receive mercy.

So why, if the first slave had received mercy, was he not able to show mercy toward another? Why had he not been transformed by the grace he had received? (The parable clearly envisages that some Christian disciples may be unforgiving in the same way, for in v. 35, the last verse of the parable, Jesus gives a stern warning to Christian disciples who do not forgive others.) I suggest the answer is that forgiveness, an expression of God's grace, is not given that people might hoard it for themselves, like a miser gloating over a large bank balance and neglecting to share the money in the bank with others. Rather, it is given as a gift to be shared and, if received as a lavish gift of un-imaginably great generosity (which is the way it is given), will always necessarily transform its recipients. I mean this: the gift can only be received in the way it is intended to be received; to receive it otherwise is merely to borrow it, until our hypocrisy and greed become evident. If people receive forgiveness in the wrong way, they do not in the end keep it; they lose what they thought they had, as it was never truly theirs. So, we see in the parable that the first slave "grabbed, and then ran" with the forgiveness he received. He looked on the forgiveness as being for his own benefit, and (to borrow the words of a board game) a "get out of jail free" card. He was selfish, and took the gift on his own terms. In the course of time, it became evident that he had received the gift otherwise than in the way it was offered and intended, and so he lost it.

This approach to forgiveness in Matthew's Gospel makes good sense psychologically and pastorally. It is experiencing undeserved grace and mercy that changes a person and enables them to be mediators of grace and mercy to others. It is true that, as in the Gospels of Mark and Luke, Matthew knows that showing grace and mercy toward another can result in the giver becoming open to the grace and mercy of God; Matt 5:7 ("blessed are the merciful, for they will receive mercy"), for example, recognizes this. So also does Matt 6:14–15, which affirms that only forgivers will themselves be forgiven. However, we need both approaches to keep the balance, and Matthew clearly knows this.

What, then, is the answer to Peter's question in 18:21, "How often should I forgive?" Jesus would say, I think, that those who have received the grace of forgiveness should forgive as lavishly as they themselves have been forgiven. The last verse of the parable makes the same point. This means people should forgive not a mere seven times (18:21) but as often as is needed, which Jesus describes as "seven times seventy [490] times." If necessary, as one friend once quipped with me when I was becoming exasperated with him, when one has forgiven 490 times, one will then have to go "the extra mile" (Matt 5:41) and forgive some more! In other words, interpersonal forgiveness is to be as lavish and generous as God's forgiveness, forgiveness that is beyond measurement and imagination.

I conclude with an observation about the implications of this parable when it comes to repentance. We have seen that being forgiven can be to experience an act of grace that will typically transform the person being forgiven. Being offered repentance can, I suggest, similarly transform the person receiving it. If this is right, not being moved to forgive if one is offered repentance is evidence of being indifferent to grace.

FORGIVENESS IN THE REST OF MATTHEW

If one takes Matthew's Gospel seriously, one cannot set forgiveness in the Christian Scriptures against the ethical teaching of the Hebrew Scriptures. As we saw in chapter 2, Jesus is clear that his teaching does not abolish or abrogate "the law and the prophets" (shorthand for much of what we now call "the Hebrew Scriptures") because, in his view, they are immutable (5:17–19). Rather, he authoritatively offers a hermeneutic of the Hebrew Scriptures from which has come the ethics of the Christian Scriptures. Christian ethics are therefore not disjoined from the ethics of the Hebrew Scriptures; they are genealogically related.

The new hermeneutic is a statement of what Jesus sees as the interpretative center of the Hebrew Scriptures. As a result, former interpretations and expressions of Jewish ethics, which come from a different hermeneutic, are sometimes defunct or given new meanings. The center of the new hermeneutic is love (5:43, and see 22:38–39), even for enemies and persecutors who can now be the subjects of love (5:44). In Matt 9:12 and 12:7 Jesus quotes Hosea 6:6 ("I desire mercy and not sacrifice"), probably to indicate that mercy and love are the epicenter of Jewish ethics, and that mercy and love trump the idea of mandatory rituals and observances. Crucial also are "justice, mercy, and faith." In consequence, the detailed legislative provisions of the law are not wrong but sometimes less "weighty" (23:23), and practicing those detailed legislative provisions must not have the effect of undermining the organizing principles of the law that Jesus sets out (23:23).

In consequence, the "tradition of the elders" sometimes has to be ignored because it contradicts the pattern of ethics that Jesus's new hermeneutic establishes (11:9–14, 15:3–6). So, defilement does not necessarily come from ignoring the law's provisions; rather, it comes from not practicing the ethics of Jesus's hermeneutic. If people are full of hate, lies, and selfishness they will be defiled, for example (15:17–20). What the scribes and Pharisees teach may be right (23:2) but it can divert people from the true purpose of the law, which Jesus says is to "produce the fruits of the kingdom" (21:43). If there is a conflict, the new ethic is to be followed. Significantly, in the parable of the Sheep and the Goats (25:31–46, and see 7:21–23), those who show love receive the kingdom. In summary and to use a modern term, Jesus "reconfigures" what it means to live as the people of God. There will be surprising consequences, as some who are assiduous law-keepers will be excluded from the kingdom (7:21–23 and 25:41–46) and others, whose law-keeping is apparently more peripheral, will be welcomed (25:31–40).

Out of Jesus's hermeneutic comes a theology of interpersonal forgiveness. People are to be loving, merciful, and just in all they do; they are not to hate or take revenge; they are to love and do good to their enemies. It is easy to see the roots of this teaching in Lev 19:17–18. In the Sermon on the Mount, for example, Jesus applauds those who are poor in spirit, meek, merciful, pure in heart, and peacemakers (5:3–9). Those who are angry are subject to judgment (5:22); rules about retribution and vengeance in the *lex talionis* (5:38) are superseded, and enemies are to be loved and prayed for (5:44). Those who do not forgive others also cut themselves away from God's forgiveness (6:14–15), because they are not producing "the fruits of the kingdom" (21:43) and are not in a frame of mind to seek and appropriate God's forgiveness.

On what basis does Jesus make these radical changes? As the religious leaders noted, Jesus was, in comparison with them, untrained and untaught. Yet he confounds them with his insights, and exposes their hypocrisy and traditionalism. Jesus says God gives him authority to do and say what he does (21:23–27). It is authenticated by miracles (e.g., 9:2–8, 11:2–6), which attest to his identity as the Messiah, Son of God, and Son of Man (e.g., 16:13–16) and to his place in the eschatological re-ordering of creation (19:28). Thus, the arguments with the Jewish leaders about what Jesus teaches and the hermeneutic he introduces are not only intra-Jewish squabbles and irritants to the Roman keepers of the peace. They are also, and principally, Christological disputes that go to the heart of who Jesus is and the mission he came to fulfil. To forgive another can therefore be a way to make a statement about what one believes about Jesus, because to forgive is to practice the ethic of the kingdom of God as Jesus formulates it.

The significance of Jesus's teaching on forgiveness in Matthew is not that Jesus establishes a new pattern of interpersonal behavior, but that he sets that pattern of behavior in a new theological and hermeneutical context. In the late Second Temple period, interpersonal forgiveness had already been identified as a species of personal ethics (see Sir 28:2);[2] it was Jesus who moved interpersonal forgiveness out of the periphery of the wisdom tradition and made it a central aspect of Jewish theology.

CONCLUSION

Matthew makes three particular contributions to the theology of forgiveness that we do not find in the other two Synoptic Gospels: first, Matthew connects God's forgiveness with Jesus's death on the cross and the covenant Jesus establishes by his death. This connection may be implicit in Mark and Luke, but the connection is not obvious. Second,

2. Cf. Bash, "Did Jesus?," 390.

Matthew modifies the pattern of forgiveness from always being "forgivers will be forgiven" to also being "the forgiven are to be forgivers." In places where the modified pattern is explored, Matthew understands forgiveness to be transformative grace, enabling people to become forgivers, in much the same way that being loved can enable people to love (as to this, see 1 John 4:19). The two patterns of forgiveness ("forgivers will be forgiven" and "the forgiven are to be forgivers") are two sides of the same coin. They are complementary, not antithetical. Last, and perhaps most significantly of all, Jesus develops a hermeneutic of the Hebrew Scriptures that provides a theological rationale for interpersonal forgiveness. People are to forgive because to forgive is one way to love God and to love people. It is a characteristic ethic—probably *the* characteristic ethic—of the kingdom of God.

QUESTIONS

1. What is Matthew's theology of forgiveness?

2. What is the significance of interpersonal forgiveness in Matthew's Gospel?

3. How is Matthew's theology of forgiveness different from Mark's?

Chapter 13

FORGIVENESS IN THE LATER CHRISTIAN SCRIPTURES

IN THIS CHAPTER, WE consider the writings of the later Christian Scriptures. Apart from in the six "disputed" Pauline letters that we have already looked at, there are explicit references to forgiveness only in the Gospel of John, First John (1 John), Hebrews, and the letter of James.

THE GOSPEL OF JOHN

The Gospel of John was put in its present form perhaps as late as the early second century CE. The emphasis in the Gospel is on love, rather than forgiveness, with forgiveness as part of what it means to love. The focus of Peter's restoration to Jesus by the Sea of Tiberias in John 21 (see vv. 15–19, especially), for example, is on whether Peter loves Jesus, not on the fact that Jesus has so obviously forgiven him. By asking Peter, "Do you love me . . . ?" Jesus implicitly means, "Do you know I love and have forgiven you, notwithstanding your three-fold denial, and do you continue to receive and accept that love which is the expression of my forgiveness?" Peter could not love Jesus if he had declined and resisted either Jesus's love or Jesus's forgiveness. Astutely, the Gospel recognizes that one cannot properly love a person one has wronged if one does not accept the forgiveness that that person offers. Equally astutely, the Gospel recognizes that one cannot forgive if one does not love or want a continuing relationship. I suspect it is not important to establish whether forgiveness precedes love or love precedes forgiveness, as forgiveness and love are interdependent.

The story of the woman caught in adultery (John 8:1–11) is, strictly speaking, not about forgiveness, though it explores a variety of responses to wrongs. It is also, almost certainly, not an original part of John's Gospel, though its profound wisdom is widely known and respected, and the story's existence (or another story resembling this one) is noted in ancient sources.

In the passage, scribes and Pharisees bring to Jesus a woman caught having an adulterous affair. They want to know whether Jesus will uphold the law's injunction in Lev 20:10 and Deut 22:22–24, and agree that she should be put to death by stoning. One reason for the question is that the religious leaders were concerned about whether Jesus disregarded the Jewish law and condoned law breaking. In effect, the question is a trap for Jesus, to see whether, by his answer, he condemns himself. The other reason is to help find out whether Jesus is (to use a modern idiom) "soft on sin" by welcoming and associating with law-breakers, and affirming that God forgives them. If this were true, he would, in the view of the scribes and Pharisees, for this reason too, stand self-condemned.

The deft outcome of the story is well known. Jesus does not directly answer the question, but asks the woman's accusers a question of his own that confronts them with their own failure to keep the law. He makes them see that, in different ways from the woman they are accusing, they are as guilty of law breaking as she. As a result, they stand self-condemned, and they realize they cannot punish the woman without acknowledging their own guilt and failure. They therefore choose to walk away.

Four implications of the story are relevant for a theology of forgiveness. The first is obviously that God's mercy and forgiveness are for all who repent, apparently regardless of the degree and nature of their sins. Second, the story shows that Jesus is not "soft on sin," for he tells the woman to "sin no more." Next, those who think they do not need God's mercy and forgiveness stand as much in need of mercy and forgiveness as egregious sinners. Judgmental, disdainful, supercilious people fool only themselves if they consider themselves to be better than those they condemn. (There are echoes here of the critical spirit of the older son in Luke 15:11–32 and of Simon the Pharisee in Luke 7:36–50 that we discussed in chapter 11.) Finally, far from neglecting and disregarding the law, Jesus upholds it by pointing all people to their sinfulness under the law, and so to their overriding need for mercy and grace.

In the context of interpersonal forgiveness, the story suggests a challenge for victims of wrongdoing. Victims need to come to terms with the fact that, sometimes, they are not so very different from those who have wronged them. Accuser and accused (as in the story), as well as victim and wrongdoer (in the case of forgiveness), sometimes each stand condemned as blameworthy, for one reason or another. When it comes to the Jewish law, Jesus says that those who are without guilt may cast the first stone. We might add, when it comes to forgiveness, only those who have not wronged others may refuse to forgive those who have wronged them.

The only explicit reference to forgiveness in John's Gospel is in 20:23. We have already briefly considered this verse in chapters 3 and 8. The text seems to presuppose an institutional setting for granting, and being assured of, divine forgiveness. The apostles broker divine forgiveness: God will forgive those they forgive, and God will retain (presumably, this means "not forgive") the sins of those whose sins the apostles retain.

It is strange that what we read about forgiveness elsewhere in the Christian Scriptures seems here to be skewed. In the Synoptic Gospels, we have seen that God will not forgive those who do not forgive others. In Paul's letters, a forgiving spirit and an approach of grace are to pervade Christian behavior. We know that God forgives all those who repent and seek forgiveness. However, at this point in John's Gospel, it appears that God will not forgive those whom the apostles do not forgive. We cannot square this circle.

FIRST JOHN

There are no explicit references to interpersonal forgiveness in First John. As we might expect, the emphasis is on love, with forgiveness implicit in the command to love (see 1 John 2:9, 11, for example).

As for divine forgiveness, we read that God forgives the sins of those who confess their sins (1 John 1:9). Given the increasingly institutional setting of forgiveness, confession of sins probably takes place not in the context of private prayer but in the setting of the public worship of a church. In 1 John 2:12, divine forgiveness comes "on account"[1] of Jesus. (A fuller translation of "on account of Jesus" is, "on account of the name of Jesus." "Name" indicates the nature of the person and personality referred to, and expresses the

1. "On account of" is the word *dia*, which is notoriously difficult to translate. With the accusative, as here, it principally denotes a causal link between two things.

person's qualities and powers. I could have translated the whole phrase as "on account of the risen power and authority of Jesus," in order to bring out the force of the word "name.") The language about Jesus's death in 1 John 1:7, 2:2, and 4:10 strongly suggests that John understood Jesus's death as an atoning sacrifice for sins that brings about forgiveness: in 1:7, John writes that "the blood of Jesus cleanses from sin" and in 2:2 and 4:10 Jesus is said to be the *hilasmos* for sins, which means the "means of appeasing" God for sins or the "sin offering" itself.[2]

JAMES

James 5:15–16 is tantalizingly difficult to interpret with certainty. The passage concerns forgiveness, though whether only divine, or divine and interpersonal, is difficult to tell.

The context seems to be to prayer generally and, in verses 14–16 in particular, to prayer with anointing for healing that church elders conduct in response to a request from an ill person. That there is a request for prayer indicates that such prayers were conducted on an *ad hoc* basis in a sick person's home on behalf of a church community that was led by an increasingly formalized hierarchy of officers.

One might want to say, on the basis of verse 15, that James links illness and unforgiven sin, and implies that sick people may be healed when they have confessed their sins and received anointing with oil at the hands of the elders.

There is some doubt about this interpretation, though the alternative is equally problematic. The alternative is that in verse 15 the elders' prayer for the ill person will result not

2. *Hilasmos* is not used elsewhere in the Christian Scriptures. John follows the late Second Temple practice of thinking that sacrifices offered under the covenant of Moses in the Hebrew Scriptures were for the forgiveness of sins. Matthew probably thought the same, and as we shall see, so does the writer to the Hebrews.

only in healing but also in salvation. (The verb for "healing" is different in vv. 15 and 16. *Sōzō* in v. 15 can be translated, "heal" or "save"; in contrast, *iaomai* in v. 16 almost always only means, "heal [from illness].") Does this mean that the elders pray for ill unbelievers? Probably not, because the context of the passage indicates James is writing to a church community of believers. "Salvation" probably means no more than healing from illness that can lead to death.

I suggest that James is conflating three discrete topics: first, the importance of prayer for the sick; second, the importance of members of the church community confessing their sins to one another; third, the increasingly formalized roles of church elders. On this basis, members of James's church confessed sins to one another, though we do not know whether they confessed their sins against God, or against one another, or both. Confession took place in a public setting. We can also say that the elders, as church leaders, were called to anoint the sick with oil, perhaps consciously following Jesus's example in Mark 6:13.

What is the value of confessing one's sins to another person or to a group of people? Practitioners of group therapy would affirm the value of being honest and straightforward about oneself in a group setting. Other members of the group can help participants explore their behavior and motives. Being open in a group setting can strengthen the resolve to distance oneself from maladaptive behavior. Others can be encouraged if they realize that they are not alone in the difficulties they face. I suspect that confessing one's sins to others in a church community setting can have similar helpful outcomes. There is, I think, great wisdom in a less individualistic approach to the forgiveness of sins that modern people tend to adopt.

HEBREWS

We do not know who wrote Hebrews or to whom Hebrews is written. We can surmise that Hebrews is almost certainly written to a community of Jewish Christians before the destruction of the temple in 70 CE. From the book, it seems that the addressees were losing confidence in the efficacy of the death of Jesus for salvation and, in the face of persecution, were at risk of giving up on their faith. In particular, the addressees were afraid that, as they were no longer participating in the temple sacrifices, they might lose their status as members of the covenant people of God. The book, probably a homily, is to assure the addressees that their fears were groundless. The writer urges them to persevere and explains to them that they have been forgiven once and for all through the death of Jesus. The writer points out that repeated offerings for sin, commanded in the Hebrew Scriptures, are no longer needed in the period of the "new covenant" (Heb 8:13), because the one offering of Jesus is eternally efficacious.

The writer treats Jesus's death as sacrificial, as does John in 1 John 1:7, 2:2, and 4:10. The writer also understands the sacrifices described in the Hebrew Scriptures as being for the forgiveness of sins (Heb 9:22). (I have already said that this reflects a development in Jewish theology during the late Second Temple period, particularly in the two centuries before the birth of Jesus.) Jesus's death, the writer also says, "perfects" those benefiting from it (Heb 10:14) and so renders future offerings for sin superfluous (Heb 10:18). The result of the atoning death of Jesus is *athetēsis* of sin: what the writer means is that as a result of Jesus's atoning death sin is set aside, removed, and annulled (Heb 9:26). The one offering of Jesus for sins (Heb 10:12) wipes from God's record all memory of human sin (Heb 10:17).

Along with 1 John 1:7, 2:2, and 4:10, these verses are the most thorough and explicit exploration of divine forgiveness in the Christian Scriptures, and one would have thought that, in the mind of the writer of Hebrews, they would form the basis of a robust theology of interpersonal forgiveness, especially given Jesus's emphasis on forgiveness in the Synoptic Gospels. Not so at all. In the exhortatory part of Hebrews, there is not a single reference to interpersonal forgiveness, even though there are appeals to "pursue peace with everyone" (Heb 12:14), to avoid bitterness (Heb 12:14), and to love one another (Heb 13:1).

Why are there not explicit references to interpersonal forgiveness in Hebrews? I suggest three possible reasons. First, the appeals to peace and love, and the appeal to avoid bitterness, could each be understood as aspects of what it means to be forgiving. At the least, the idea of forgiveness is not incompatible with these exhortations. Next, it might be that interpersonal forgiveness is not a pressing topic for the community to which the writer addresses the homily. Last, the writer might share the traditional reluctance of the Jews (a reluctance to which I alluded in chapter 2), to recognize that human beings, as well as God, can forgive.

SOME FINAL OBSERVATIONS

In some of the later writings of the Christian Scriptures, we see an increasingly institutionalized approach to forgiveness. The apostles are brokers of divine forgiveness; church elders pray for and anoint the sick, who may be ill because of unconfessed sin; confession of sin can take place in a corporate setting.

We should note too that there are relatively few references to interpersonal forgiveness. As I have suggested, this is principally because, by the time of the later Christian Scriptures, love is the organizing principle of Christian ethics, with forgiveness assumed to be an expression of what it means to love. Whereas in the Synoptic Gospels interpersonal forgiveness is identified as integral to salvation (as in the Lord's Prayer, for example), the later traditions in the Christian Scriptures replace interpersonal forgiveness with love as the prerequisite for salvation. The emphasis on grace in forgiveness, so powerful in Paul's writings, has also receded. None of this should be taken as suggesting that by this time forgiveness no longer matters; rather, forgiveness has been rightly set in the second part of the "greatest commandment" (Matt 22:37–40).

Both Hebrews (probably pre-70 CE) and First John (probably early second century CE) understand Jesus's death to be an atoning sacrifice for sins. Hebrews gives a sustained exploration of divine forgiveness, offering a midrash (interpretive exegesis) of the (in)efficacy of the Jewish sacrificial system in comparison with superior effects of the sacrificial death of Jesus. The writer does not draw any inferences about interpersonal forgiveness from this, but does exhort the Hebrew Christians, on the basis of the atoning death of Christ and its effects, not to abandon their faith.

QUESTIONS

1. What is the theology of forgiveness in the Gospel of John and First John?

2. Explain theologically the statement, "Only those who have not wronged others may refuse to forgive those who have wronged them."

3. What do we learn about forgiveness in the letter of James?

4. What does Hebrews contribute to an understanding of divine and interpersonal forgiveness?

PART 3

FURTHER QUESTIONS

Chapter 14

FORGIVENESS AND JUSTICE

You may be familiar with the expression "the elephant in the room." The expression refers to something obvious that is being deliberately ignored or left unaddressed, usually because it would be embarrassing, awkward, or unwelcome to address it. Just as it would be impossible to overlook the fact of an elephant in a room, the expression points to the absurdity of trying to ignore something that is on the minds of all present but which they do not want to talk about.

So far, in this book, there has been an "elephant in the room." (I can't bring myself to write that there is "an elephant in the book"!) The "elephant" is the fact that forgiveness is sometimes seen as being fundamentally unjust because, as we have seen, interpersonal forgiveness usually involves victims relinquishing, and so (one might say) sacrificing, their rights against wrongdoers. The resulting injustice is twofold. First, a victim, V, will lose hope for recompense and redress for the wrongs V has suffered.[1] Sec-

---

1. Altogether different, of course, are the occasions when one wishes voluntarily to forgo any entitlement to or expectation of justice, perhaps to spare oneself further hurt, pain, or difficulty. This often amounts to choosing to walk away from a situation, to cut one's losses, and get on with life.

ond, wrongdoers will escape the punishment they deserve. The "winners" in this situation, so people suggest, are the wrongdoers, and the "losers" are the victims—doubly so, first on account of having been wronged, and second on account of being left with their losses. Expressed this way, who would want to forgive?

Even though it is unpalatable, there is some truth in this description of forgiveness. As we have seen, forgiveness is a sacrificial act of love that involves loss to a victim. There is also no escaping the fact that Christian theology recognizes there is a duty on V to show love and mercy to a wrongdoer, W, notwithstanding that W has violated V, and even though this may mean that victims show to wrongdoers the very qualities that the wrongdoers failed to show to their victims.

However, and in counterbalance, Christian theology affirms the place of justice as a correlate of love, albeit sometimes in uneasy alliance.[2] When it comes to forgiveness, Christian theology recognizes that, in addition to V's duty to show love and mercy to W, V has a privilege, namely, that V should hope for and receive a measure of justice, in recompense for having been wronged. In this context I take justice at least to be that W reciprocates V's view that V has been wronged, and that W does what W can to make restitution to V.

When people forgive, how do the Christian Scriptures balance the two disparate elements of love and justice?

REPENTANCE AND FORGIVENESS

If forgiveness is to be substantially just, W needs to demonstrate remorse, contrition, and repentance; W also needs to

---

2. Bash, *Ethics*, 154–56; Bash, *Just Forgiveness*; Philpott, "Justice and Forgiveness."

make reparation when it is possible to do so. (This suggestion fits the pattern of forgiveness in the Gospels where, almost always, repentance precedes forgiveness.) Actions and responses such as these demonstrate that W has judged W's own actions, and sought to put right what can be put right. Of course, this still leaves open the question how much repentance is necessary, and who determines whether the repentance is genuine. Nevertheless, acknowledging one's wrongdoing and seeking to put right what one can are a form of voluntary, self-imposed justice in relation to the wrong that one has done.

These observations take us to the heart of what has been something of storm-center of Christian theology for close on the last half millennium as well as in the early years of the church, namely, the nature of God's grace in Christian salvation and practice. We now explore the question of grace, and its relationship to repentance and forgiveness, by asking three questions.

First, does insisting on repentance compromise the idea of forgiveness as being a loving gift, freely given, that is, of forgiveness as being a gift of grace given without preconditions? Paul's view would be that it would. So, for example, Paul does not insist on repentance as a prerequisite of justification. For Paul, justification is a gift of grace without reference to "works," including repentance, or law-keeping. (Paul rarely mentions repentance; when he does, he sees it as a response to grace, not a means to grace, as, for example, in Rom 2:4.) However, in other parts of the Christian Scriptures as we have seen, forgiveness is not always given without preconditions. In the Synoptic Gospels, for example, repentance appears to be mandatory before God will forgive and, as we have seen in both versions of the Lord's Prayer, God's forgiveness of an individual depends on that individual forgiving others.

Second, do we compromise the idea of forgiveness as a gift of grace, if we say that forgiveness results in reciprocal obligations on the recipient of forgiveness? We do, if grace means a gift, freely given to the recipient without obligations in response. However, in some parts of the Christian Scriptures, forgiveness does carry reciprocal obligations, as we saw, for example, in the parable of the Unjust Servant in Matt 18:23–35.

Third, is V obliged to forgive W (that is, to give a gift of grace), if W is repentant? If we say, "Yes," and insist that, because it is loving to forgive, V should forgive W if W is repentant, we compromise the voluntary, gift-like quality of forgiveness. If we say, "No," we preserve the gift-like quality of forgiveness. However, this fails to take account of some strands of Christian tradition that suggest that grace—and so forgiveness—will be given if preconditions are met, and that grace (and forgiveness) continue if consequential obligations (such as forgiving others) are heeded.

We cannot resolve the difficulties, because they reflect an unresolved debate within the Christian Scriptures about the preconditions for and consequences of the grace of God's forgiveness.

JUSTICE, JUDGEMENT, AND FORGIVENESS

These observations still leave open the question, "Can forgiveness be just?" if the result of forgiving means that one no more than accepts the repentance, remorse, and perhaps also the reparation of W. We seek a solution by looking at the reasons Paul gives for saying that divine forgiveness is just, and then asking whether Paul's answer is of help when it comes to interpersonal forgiveness.

We begin with a surprising observation: in the undisputed letters, Paul explicitly refers to divine forgiveness in only one verse (Rom 4:7, in a quotation from Ps 32:1 in the Septuagint). However, though only mentioned in one verse, divine forgiveness is integral to Paul's thought, because those to whom God has "reckoned righteousness" (Rom 4:6) and against whom God "will not reckon sin" (Rom 4:8) are forgiven and their sins "covered" (Rom 4:7). In other words, and despite the paucity of explicit references to it, justified people are forgiven people.

From Rom 4:7, we have a clue to what Paul understands divine forgiveness to be. In the verse, Paul quotes the Greek version of Ps 32:1. The quoted passage celebrates God's forgiveness in three phrases. The first is with the verb *aphiēmi*, in the sense of "let go" or "release." The other two phrases are examples of "synonymous parallelism," which means that by each of the three phrases, the same idea is expressed in different words, with each phrase explaining and perhaps even elaborating the others. The two phrases are that God "covers" sins and that God will "not reckon against" people their sins. Put together, the three phrases all express the idea that forgiveness means that God completely removes human sin from God's record and memory.

Paul implicitly recognizes the dilemma of how forgiveness can be both loving and just. The dilemma is starkly in evidence in Rom 3:25 where, in a context similar to justification, Paul uses the noun *paresis* to describe God "passing over" sin. More fully, the word means deliberately disregarding something by letting it go unpunished. The dilemma of Rom 3:25 is this: God, who is loving, apparently unjustly passes over and leaves sin unpunished.

Paul offers a solution that resolves the dilemma with reference to his confidence in the integrity and self-consistency of God. He does this in Rom 3:21–26, for example, insisting that God out of grace gives salvation as a gift to undeserving people, and that by the atonement God "proves" that God is righteous, thereby satisfying the demands of justice. (Paul does the same in Rom 9–11, when he agonizes over the fact that Jewish people seem to be rejecting the gospel and salvation in Christ.) Implicit in Paul's thinking is an assumption that divine justice accords with what human beings mean by "justice" and with what, from a human point of view, is morally right.

In Paul's view, "justification" and the atonement are just because God is "righteous." The words "justification" and "righteous" are etymologically related in Greek and have at their root the idea of "rightness" and justice. In Paul's thought, because God is righteous, God can only act righteously. It follows, so Paul continues, that God's "justification" is necessarily just and that when God justifies, there is no conflict between God's love and God's justice.

However, if we stop for a moment, we will see quickly that Paul's argument, which is based on the semantic interrelationship of the words "just," "justice," "justification," and "righteousness" in Greek, is largely circular and based on faith-based assertions. The argument runs something like this: since God is loving and just, God's justification (and so forgiveness) are therefore loving and just.

Paul does have some "evidence" for his assertions. He recognizes that God is forbearing and loving because, instead of destroying sinful humanity in judgment, God saves it through the atoning death of Christ, an atoning death that demonstrates, in Paul's view, that God does not compromise his justice (e.g., Rom 3:25, 5:8). He recognizes another way that God is just: notwithstanding forgiveness, God holds people to account for their actions because each person, including those who have been justified and forgiven, will give an account of their actions to God in a judgment of works (Rom 14:10–12 and 2 Cor 5:10).

On this last point, we face what appears to be another paradox: people are justly forgiven ("justified") and their sins both "passed over" (Rom 3:25) and not "reckoned" against them, yet they will be "accountable" to God for what they have done. How can their sins be "passed over" and not counted against them, yet they remain accountable for them? Paul does not address the paradox, and leaves it apparently unnoticed.

If he had seen it, Paul might try to explain the paradox in this way. He seems to draw a distinction between the "old self" and (though he does not use this term) the "new self" or (as in 2 Cor 5:17 and Gal 6:15) the "new creation." He might say that it is the "old self" that gives account for sin. The "new self" lives with Christ, who gives "life" to mortal bodies (Rom 8:11), and is spared "condemnation" (Rom 8:1). If this is the solution to the paradox, there is no escaping the dualism in Paul's thought at this point. Nevertheless, the explanation does enable us to explain how God can be both loving (forgiving people their sins and not holding them to account) and just (holding them to account for their sins) at the same time.

Why does Paul say relatively little about forgiveness? I suggest that a reason for the paucity of explicit references to forgiveness in Paul's thought, besides the reasons I suggested in chapter 9, is that Paul knew that the gift of divine forgiveness and the gift of interpersonal forgiveness depend on antecedent repentance and result in consequential obligations. In Paul's view, these conditions compromise the nature of grace, as Paul understands it. For Paul, a better way of explaining salvation and ethics—a way that in Paul's mind does not compromise the centrality of grace—is by a theology of justification, not forgiveness.

Returning to the whether forgiveness can be just, I conclude that the pattern of justice embedded in divine forgiveness that Paul identifies does not help us identify how interpersonal forgiveness might also be construed as just. The most persuasive answer I can offer is the one already suggested earlier in this chapter: wrongdoers who repent, who are contrite and remorseful, and who (when appropriate) offer reparation demonstrate that they themselves have judged their actions and sought to put right what they can. They stand (as it were) self-condemned, and their self-imposed sentence is to admit and acknowledge the wrong and do what they can to restore the *status quo ante*. Nothing can fully "put back the clock," but wrongdoers can use their best endeavors to put things right. This, it seems to me, is good enough justice.

There is now, no longer, an "elephant in the room."

QUESTIONS

1. To what extent is forgiveness unjust?
2. How does Christian theology address the supposed injustice of forgiveness?
3. Explain why Paul says relatively little about forgiveness.

Chapter 15

MODERN-DAY FORGIVENESS

THIS CHAPTER, THE CONCLUDING chapter of the book, offers some further reflections about interpersonal forgiveness in its contemporary context.

THEOLOGICAL INDIFFERENCE?

Interpersonal forgiveness has long been regarded as one of the defining characteristics of Christian ethics. Surprisingly then, there has been little critical reflection about interpersonal forgiveness within the Christian tradition. Interpersonal forgiveness has tended to be taken as a given, self-evident to all people of reason and faith. Instead, divine forgiveness and the atonement have been center stage of academic endeavor. It seems as if discussion about interpersonal forgiveness has been tacked on to major treatises on the atonement, almost as an afterthought. If divine forgiveness is center stage, interpersonal forgiveness seems no more than a member of the chorus.

Of course, there are exceptions. In 1718, Joseph Butler preached two sermons on forgiveness in the Rolls Chapel, Chancery Lane, in London. The sermons have been influential in setting the starting point for the modern discussion of forgiveness, and at various points in this book I have discussed aspects of the sermons. Hugh Ross Mackintosh wrote an important book in 1927 entitled *The Christian Experience of Forgiveness*. L. Gregory Jones's 1995 monograph *Embodying Forgiveness* is another important book with interpersonal forgiveness in the Christian tradition as its principal focus, nearly seventy years later. Between these two points, there were some other contributions to the study of interpersonal forgiveness, but as I have said, most of these contributions were either principally popular works or adjuncts to studies on the atonement.

In the latter part of the twentieth century, forgiveness became a topic of academic, secular discourse, particularly in some branches of philosophy, psychology, and political science. Jeffrie Murphy and Jean Hampton's *Forgiveness and Mercy* (1988) remains a seminal contribution among philosophers. Christian critical reflection on the topic still remained relatively meager at this time, and continues to be so. This is regrettable, because (as I hope this book has shown) Christian theology has an important contribution to make to secular, academic reflection about forgiveness; the insights of some secular scholars also have an important contribution to make to a subtler and more nuanced theology of forgiveness also, as I hope this book has shown.

PUBLIC FORUMS FOR FORGIVENESS AND RECONCILIATION

Among some, there is unease about language to do with forgiveness being used in secular, public forums. Forgiveness is sometimes perceived to be a "faith" concept, and a "Christian" faith concept in particular. The perception that forgiveness is an especially "Christian" virtue has, rightly or wrongly, been reinforced by some of the widely circulated statements Archbishop Tutu made during and after the Truth and Reconciliation Commission in South Africa. Earlier in this book, I have shown that the contemporary view of forgiveness as a "Christian concept" is an oversimplification, and in other publications I have shown that forgiveness has its origins in secular, as well as in Judeo-Christian thought.[1]

People prefer to speak of reconciliation, as reconciliation seems to them to be a more faith-neutral concept to use. The result has been the development of several new disciplines that focus on how best to promote reconciliation and restoration between communities and groups in conflict: these disciplines include conflict management, conflict resolution, conflict transformation, and preventive negotiation. In international relations, the new disciplines are usually part of what is today called "transitional justice." The models that are used generally treat religious views and convictions as being private and personal, with no relevance or application to peacemaking and reconciliation in a public forum.[2]

Nevertheless, the drive to promote restored relations between previously estranged groups is at the heart of Christian theology and practice, since restoration and reconciliation are integral to the atonement. Not surprisingly, therefore, some contemporary Christian groups, such as the Quakers and Mennonites, see part of their ministry as being to promote peace, conflict resolution, and reconciliation through the work of mediators. So also do some individuals. Notable in the Anglican (Episcopal) Church is the Archbishop of Canterbury, Justin Welby, who has experience of facilitating conflict resolution in Africa. In South Africa,

1. See Bash, "Spirituality," 62–63.
2. Kubálková, "International Political Theology."

individuals, especially from Christian faith traditions, as well as churches institutionally have had a significant role in facilitating conflict resolution and peace.[3]

Restored relations usually come about through the work of mediators. The Christian Scriptures contain examples of mediators who bring about reconciliation. For example, in Heb 8:6, 9:15, and 12:24, Jesus is described as "the mediator" of a new and better covenant that reconciles humanity to God. In 1Tim 2:5 Jesus is said to be "the mediator" between God and humanity. Other agents can also be mediators of a divine covenant: Moses is described as the mediator of the covenant at Sinai (Gal 3:19) and Paul understands his apostolic role as being a "ministry of reconciliation" (2 Cor 5:18) with a "message of reconciliation" (2 Cor 5:19).

There is, of course, a significant difference between Jesus's mediatorial role (which does not involve any element of negotiation or compromise) and an interpersonal mediatorial role (which almost always involves the estranged parties negotiating and compromising). This may perhaps explain what Paul means in Gal 3:20, namely, that the covenant Jesus mediated involved only "one party," in the sense the covenant was not for negotiation and compromise. Nevertheless, we can still expect Christians to celebrate taking on the task of being mediators and so promoting reconciliation, because not only is reconciliation integral to the atonement but also three great biblical figures, Moses, Jesus, and Paul, were mediators who promoted reconciliation.

3. For more on contemporary religious support for peace-building, see Appleby, *Ambivalence*; Thomas, *Global Resurgence*, 173–96; and Gopin, *Between Eden*.

"NEW" TYPES OF FORGIVENESS

Two "new" types of forgiveness are sometimes talked about in public affairs: invitational forgiveness and political forgiveness. They both bear some of the hallmarks of the sort of forgiveness rooted in the Christian Scriptures that I have been describing; however, they are also different in important respects, and have been adapted for a modern, political context.

Invitational forgiveness is a form of forgiveness individuals or groups can offer or receive. The aim is to promote peace, justice, and restoration by the offer of "forgiveness." An example of invitational forgiveness might be the magnanimity of Nelson Mandela toward his former oppressors that became the trigger for a significant measure of political reconciliation and healing. One suspects that without that magnanimity, the outcome of the release of Mandela from prison might have been profoundly divisive for the future of South Africa.

The second form of "new" forgiveness is called "political forgiveness." By this is meant a public offer of forgiveness expressing the intention no longer to hold community leaders and the communities they represent liable for past actions, usually of the communities' forbears. The aim is to bring about institutional or public restoration between communities in conflict. Public statements of remorse for forbears' misplaced actions can be covert appeals for political forgiveness.

"MUDDLED FORGIVENESS"

At least three problems typically occur when people think, write, and talk about forgiveness.

In my view, on occasions, what people say can be well meant, but not well grounded. An example of wrongly grounded forgiveness is when onlookers, often who are well meaning, urge victims to forgive because they (the onlookers) regard forgiveness as a virtuous end in itself, without regard to issues of justice and integrity. Forgiveness is therefore sometimes regarded as lacking in focus and clarity, not worth rigorous study. I hope this book makes clear that, though unanswered questions remain, forgiveness is anything but confused and vague.

Second, in some modern discussions, especially in political affairs, discussion about "reconciliation" has been broad enough to include what we have called in this book "forgiveness," and vice versa. Some of Archbishop Tutu's comments during and after the Truth and Reconciliation Commission in South Africa, for example, illustrate that he explicitly conflated forgiveness with one of the statutorily defined aspirations of the Commission, namely, reconciliation. Confusion about these two discrete, though related, ideas makes them less useful in discussion and practice, because in their conflated form they include so much that needs to be considered separately. Having said this, the same confusion may be evident in the Christian Scriptures. In Matt 5:23–24, for example, worshippers are not to offer sacrifices until they are "reconciled" to people from whom they have been estranged. I think that reconciliation in this context presupposes forgiveness.

Last, forgiveness and reconciliation have become "catch-all" ideas, embracing more or less anything to do with restoring relationships in whichever ways people want or think might be helpful. When people decide it is time to end conflict, they are likely to agree on the benefit of also restoring their relationships; they are unlikely to disagree, if they can pick and choose the outcome they want and how to attain it. Only when they get together and begin the hard work of trying to resolve the conflict will it become clear that they do not know or agree on what they need to do, be, or change to get to the outcome they want. A clear demarcation of the discrete ideas, processes, and concepts for restoring relationships is essential if people and groups in conflict are to be empowered to resolve their differences.

THE FUTURE OF FORGIVENESS

At various points in this book I have sought to put a "hedge" around forgiveness and suggested that forgiveness, if we are to hold true to its biblical expressions, should be more tightly drawn than sometimes it is today. However, I would like to add an important rider to what I have just said: modern reformulations of forgiveness for new settings and with new contours can successfully result in the restoration of fractured relationships, as well as reconciliation between individuals and communities. This can be so, whether or not the reformulations of forgiveness fully conform to the paradigms of forgiveness explored in the Christian Scriptures. Christian theology is not the arbiter of what is or is not forgiveness, though it has much to give to a richly textured description of forgiveness.

A biblically rooted theology of the atonement will emphasize that the outcomes of the atonement can be forgiveness, reconciliation, and restoration. Human endeavor that promotes these ends reflects the goal of the atonement, and is to be celebrated and practiced as a God-given task for human beings in their own vocations. The limitations to the scope of forgiveness that I have suggested (such as, for example, repentance and a mutual desire for restoration) are necessary for a biblically rooted theology of forgiveness, since not all that feels like forgiveness is biblically shaped forgiveness. Nevertheless, many Christians rightly promote and take part in dialogue and processes to help bring about an end to conflict and division, even if contemporary views of and approaches to these outcomes do not always sit entirely congruent with what we read in the Christian Scriptures. Just because one cannot have it all one's own way does not mean one should take one's bat home.

It is easy to fail to understand the viewpoints, history, and hurts of others if you ignore those people. It is easy for your enemy to remain in ignorance about your suffering and grief about the past if you do not speak to your enemy. It is unwise to undervalue mechanisms that enable divided people and groups to come together, because the mechanisms or their anticipated outcomes do not satisfy our intellectual or faith categories. Only with generosity of spirit toward the views, needs, and starting points of others can there be hope for restoration and reconciliation. If forgiveness in its biblically shaped form results too, so much the better.

QUESTIONS

1. Distinguish between "invitational forgiveness," "political forgiveness," and "muddled forgiveness."

2. Can you suggest reasons why interpersonal forgiveness in relatively understated in modern theological writings?

3. Suggest reasons why Christians should be active in seeking peace and reconciliation in secular contexts.

BIBLIOGRAPHY

Allison, Dale C. "It Don't Come Easy: A History of Disillusionment." In *Jesus, Criteria, and the Demise of Authenticity*, edited by Chris Keith and Anthony Le Donne, 186–99. London: T. & T. Clark International, 2012.

Appleby, R. Scott. *The Ambivalence of the Sacred: Religion, Violence, and Reconciliation*. Oxford: Rowan & Littlefield, 2000.

Arendt, Hannah. *The Human Condition*. Chicago: University of Chicago Press, 1958.

Bailey, Daniel P. "Jesus as the Mercy Seat: The Semantics and Theology of Paul's Use of *Hilasterion* in Romans 3:25." *Tyndale Bulletin* 51 (2000) 155–58.

Barbour, Robert S. *Tradition-Historical Criticism of the Gospels*. Studies in Creative Criticism 4. London: SPCK, 1972.

Bash, Anthony. "Did Jesus Discover Forgiveness?" *Journal of Religious Ethics* 41 (2013) 382–99.

———. "Forgiveness: A Re-Appraisal." *Studies in Christian Ethics* 24 (2011) 1–14.

———. *Forgiveness and Christian Ethics*. New Studies in Christian Ethics 29. Cambridge: Cambridge University Press, 2007.

———. "Forgiveness, Reconciliation and Spirituality: A Theological Perspective." *Journal for the Study of Spirituality* 4 (2014) 58–72.

———. *Just Forgiveness: Exploring the Bible, Weighing the Issues*. London: SPCK, 2011.

Brudholm, Thomas. *Resentment's Virtue: Jean Améry and the Refusal to Forgive*. Philadelphia: Temple University Press, 2008.

Butler, Joseph. "Fifteen Sermons Preached at the Rolls' Chapel." In *The Works of Joseph Butler*, edited by William E. Gladstone, 136–67. Vol. 2, "Sermons." Reprint, Bristol: Thoemmes, 1995.

Chadwick, Henry. *The Church in Ancient Society: From Galilee to Gregory the Great*. Oxford: Oxford University Press, 2001.

Corley, Jeremy. *Sirach*. New Collegeville Bible Commentary 21. Collegeville, MN: Liturgical, 2013.

Derrida, Jacques. *On Cosmopolitanism and Forgiveness*. Translated by Mark Dooley and Michael Hughes, with a preface by Simon Critchley and Richard Kearney. London: Routledge, 2001.

Evans, Christopher F. *Saint Luke*. New ed. with a preface by Robert Morgan and Michael Wolter. London: SCM, 2008.

Garrard, Eve, and David McNaughton. *Forgiveness*. Durham, UK: Acumen, 2010.

Gopin, Marc. *Between Eden and Armageddon: The Future of World Religions, Violence, and Peacemaking*. New York: Oxford University Press, 2000.

Gorman, Michael, J. *Cruciformity: Paul's Narrative Spirituality of the Cross*. Grand Rapids: Eerdmans, 2001.

Griswold, Charles L. *Forgiveness: A Philosophical Exploration*. Cambridge: Cambridge University Press, 2007.

Haber, Joram G. *Forgiveness*. Savage, MD: Rowman and Littlefield, 1991.

Harbsmeier, Christoph. "Forgiveness and Forbearance in Ancient China." In *The Ethics of Forgiveness: A Collection of Essays*, edited by Christel Fricke, 13–29. New York: Routledge, 2011.

Holmgren, Margaret R. *Forgiveness and Retribution: Responding to Wrongdoing*. New York: Cambridge University Press, 2012.

Hooker, Morna D. "Christology and Methodology." *New Testament Studies* 17 (1970) 480–87.

———. *From Adam to Christ: Essays on Paul*. Cambridge: Cambridge: University Press, 1990.

———. "On Using the Wrong Tool." *Theology* 75 (1972) 570–81.

Johansson, Daniel. "'Who Can Forgive Sins but God Alone?' Human and Angelic Agents, and Divine Forgiveness in Early Judaism." *Journal for the Study of the New Testament* 33 (2011) 351–74.

Jones, L. Gregory. *Embodying Forgiveness: A Theological Analysis*. Grand Rapids: Eerdmans, 1995.

Josephus, Titus Flavius. *Jewish Antiquities*. Translated by H. St. J. Thackeray et al. Loeb Classical Library. 6 vols. Cambridge: Harvard University Press, 1930.

Kant, Immanuel. *The Metaphysics of Morals: Practical Philosophy*. Translated and edited by Mary Gregor with an introduction by Roger J. Sullivan. New York: Cambridge University Press, 1996.

Konstan, David. "Assuaging Rage: Remorse, Repentance, and Forgiveness in the Classical World." In *Ancient Forgiveness: Classical, Judaic, and Christian*, edited by Charles L. Griswold and David Konstan, 17–30. Cambridge: Cambridge University Press, 2012.

————. *Before Forgiveness: The Origins of a Moral Idea*. Cambridge: Cambridge University Press, 2010.

Kselman, John S. "Forgiveness." In *The Anchor Bible Dictionary*, edited by David N. Freeman et al., 2:835–38. New York: Doubleday, 1992.

Kubálková, Vendulka. "Towards an International Political Theology." In *Religion in International Relations: The Return from Exile*, edited by Fabio Petito and Pavlos Hatzopoulos, 79–105. New York: Palgrave Macmillan, 2003.

Lapsley, Michael. *Redeeming the Past: My Journey from Freedom Fighter to Healer*. With Stephen Karakashian. Maryknoll: Orbis, 2012.

Mackintosh, Hugh Ross. *The Christian Experience of Forgiveness*. London: Nisbet, 1927.

Marcus, Joel. *Mark 1–8: A New Translation with Introduction and Commentary*. New York: Doubleday, 2000.

Metzger, Bruce M. *A Textual Commentary on the Greek New Testament: A Companion Volume to the United Bible Societies' Greek New Testament*. 3rd ed. New York: United Bible Societies, 1971.

Milgrom, Jacob. *Leviticus 1–16: A New Translation with Introduction and Commentary*. Anchor Bible 3. New York: Doubleday, 1989.

Minas, Anne C. "God and Forgiveness." *Philosophical Quarterly* 25 (1975) 138–50.

Morgan, Michael L. "Mercy, Repentance, and Forgiveness." In *Ancient Forgiveness: Classical, Judaic, and Christian*, edited by Charles L. Griswold and David Konstan, 137–57. Cambridge: Cambridge University Press, 2012.

Murphy, Jeffrie G. *Getting Even: Forgiveness and Its Limits*. New York: Oxford University Press, 2003.

Murphy, Jeffrie G., and Jean Hampton. *Forgiveness and Mercy*. Cambridge: Cambridge University Press, 1988.

Nietzsche, Friedrich W. *Thus Spake Zarathustra: A Book for Everyone and No One*. Translated with an introduction by R. J. Hollingdale. Harmondsworth: Penguin, 1969.

Parkinson, "Lou Vincent": The Most Brutal Form of Apology," *BBC*, July 4, 2014, http://www.bbc.co.uk/news/magazine-28106549.

Philpott, Daniel. "The Justice of Forgiveness." *Journal of Religious Ethics* 41 (2013) 400–416.

Sakenfield, Katherine D. "The Problem of Divine Forgiveness in Numb. 14." *Catholic Biblical Quarterly* 37 (1975) 317–30.

Sanders, Ed P. *Paul and Palestinian Judaism: A Comparison of Patterns of Religion*. Philadelphia: Fortress, 1977.

Snaith, John G. *Ecclesiasticus, or the Wisdom of Jesus Son of Sirach.* Cambridge Bible Commentary. Cambridge: Cambridge University Press, 1974.

Thomas, Scott M. *The Global Resurgence of Religion and the Transformation of International Relations: The Struggle for the Soul of the Twenty-First Century.* New York: Palgrave Macmillan, 2005.

Waal, Frans B. M. de. *Chimpanzee Politics: Power and Sex among Apes.* London: Jonathan Cape, 1982.

Wittgenstein, Ludwig. *Philosophical Investigations.* Translated by G. E. M. Anscombe. 2nd ed. Oxford: Blackwell, 1958.

SUBJECT INDEX

SCRIPTURE INDEX

Made in the USA
Middletown, DE
10 August 2021

45777359R00102